REBUILD MY CHURCH

D1596404

REBUILD MY
CHURCH

God's Plan for Authentic Catholic Renewal

ALAN SCHRECK, PH.D.

PUBLISHED BY ST. ANTHONY MESSENGER PRESS
CINCINNATI, OHIO

RESCRIPT

In accord with the *Code of Canon Law*, I hereby grant my permission to publish *Rebuild My Church: God's Plan for Authentic Catholic Renewal*.

Most Reverend R. Daniel Conlon

Bishop

Diocese of Steubenville

Steubenville, Ohio

February 11, 2010

The permission to publish is a declaration that a book or pamphlet is considered to be free of doctrinal or moral error. It is not implied that those who have granted the permission to publish agree with the contents, opinions or statements expressed.

Unless otherwise noted, Scripture passages have been taken from the *Revised Standard Version*, Catholic edition. Copyright 1946, 1952, 1971 by the Division of Christian Education of the National Council of Churches of Christ in the USA. Used by permission. All rights reserved. Note: The editors of this volume have made minor changes in capitalization to some of the Scripture quotations herein. Please consult the original source for proper capitalization.

Excerpts from *Enthusiasm: A Chapter in the History of Religion,* by Ronald Knox, copyright © 1950, used by permission of A P Watt Ltd on behalf of The Earl of Oxford and Asquith.

Vatican II quotations are taken from Austin Flannery, ed., *Vatican Council II: The Conciliar and Post Conciliar Documents, New Revised Edition,* vol. 1, copyright 1996, Costello Publishing Company, Northport, New York.

Novo Millennio Ineunte and *Christifidelis Laici* quotations are taken from the Vatican Web site, www.vatican.va.

Cover and book design by Mark Sullivan
Cover image © istockphoto.com/Alexander Klemm

LIBRARY OF CONGRESS CATALOGING-IN-PUBLICATION DATA
Schreck, Alan.
Rebuild my church : God's plan for authentic Catholic renewal / Alan Schreck.
p. cm.
Includes bibliographical references and index.
ISBN 978-0-86716-947-8 (pbk. : alk. paper) 1. Church renewal—Catholic Church. I. Title.
BX1746.S295 2010
262'.02—dc22
2010001145

ISBN 978-0-86716-947-8

Copyright ©2010, Alan Schreck. All rights reserved.

Published by Servant Books, an imprint of St. Anthony Messenger Press.
28 W. Liberty St.
Cincinnati, OH 45202
www.ServantBooks.org

Printed in the United States of America.

Printed on acid-free paper.

10 11 12 13 14 5 4 3 2 1

All glory, praise, and thanksgiving be given to
God the Holy Spirit,
who with gentleness, mercy, and might
constantly renews the Church!

CONTENTS

NOTE TO THE READER

In order to present a broad view of church renewal in the Catholic tradition, particular chapters of this book may be of greater interest to different audiences. The first, second, and seventh (final) chapters are more practical and pastoral, and may be of general interest to all readers. Chapter three contains a more in-depth theological analysis of church renewal, while chapters four, five, and (especially) six involve more detailed historical material and analysis.

PREFACE

Why a book on church renewal?

For me it's another way of telling the "story" of Catholicism. A catechism describes what Catholics believe, the Vatican II documents tell how the Catholic church understands and presents herself today, and a history of the church covers everything else. (I've written a book on each of these.) Through all this the church is in a constant state of renewal, as she responds to the Holy Spirit in each age and situation.

The Holy Spirit offers the grace of renewal to individuals as well as to the church. With that grace amazing things are possible. Indeed, a Christian's life cannot advance in union with God without that grace.

My own life provides a case in point. For most of my freshman year of college, I was practicing my faith but in an agonizing search for God. The Lord, in his goodness, revealed himself through an incredible outpouring of the Holy Spirit in my life. Through the grace of the charismatic renewal, I came to understand that Catholicism was more than a religion of ritual. Fortunately, a theologically solid priest on campus—a Thomist theology professor—understood this too and welcomed the use of the charisms in a regular weekday Mass in a university chapel.

Vatican II taught that the charisms (listed by St. Paul in 1 Corinthians 12 and 14) are to be received and used with joy and thanksgiving for the building up of the church. But it took (and is still taking) time for the church to adjust to and respond to these graces as God is renewing them in fact and not just in a church document.

Speaking of Vatican II, it amazes me that while I had not read those documents back in my freshman year of college, I quickly came to understand and experience many of the most important points of the council's teaching. In fact, it would not be exaggerating too much to say that "everything I needed to know about Vatican II I learned (by grace, in an 'infused' way) when the Holy Spirit burst into my life."

I knew what it meant to say that Jesus is the Lord—that he is the center and Savior of all things: of the world, the church, and my life. I knew that I, even as a layperson, was called to holiness, and I knew that prayer was essential to growth in faith and holiness. It was almost impossible *not* to participate fully and actively in the liturgy and sacraments, where I encountered Jesus in a new way, and to use the charisms I had received (for example, glossolalia and prophecy) to worship the Lord and to build up others in the church, as St. Paul taught.

Sacred Scripture "came alive," and I wanted to read and study it. My experience of the Spirit "inoculated" me against the nonsense of biblical scholarship that wanted to deny the real power of God to convert, heal, and do other mighty works. This was very important when I later began to study theology and went on to write a master's thesis on a New Testament theme.

I knew that I needed others in the church to help me grow in my faith; the church as a living communion of the people of God became a daily lived reality for me. I knew that I was called to be involved in the mission of Christ and the church: I *had* to share my faith with others—how could I keep this Good News to myself?—and to serve others. (No, this renewal did not produce a solipsistic escape from the world nor a "holy club" oblivious to the needs of others.)

The grace of this renewal even enabled me to understand the beauty of celibacy, religious life, and the priesthood, and to appreciate and respect the role of the hierarchy in guiding the church and promoting its renewal. How blessed we were to have Pope Paul VI, and later John Paul II, who really understood and fostered genuine renewal!

So the heart of the teaching of Vatican II, though I had never read the documents, was part of my life. Is it any wonder that when many responsible theologians and renewal leaders are asked, "What can we do to renew the church?" they say, "Pray that people receive an outpouring of the Holy Spirit!"? When the Holy Spirit comes in power into a person's life, the church and her teachings "make sense" and can be lived. That person in turn is likely to become an agent of true renewal. "For the kingdom of God does not consist in talk but in power" (1 Corinthians 4:20).

However, be warned: If you say things like this, you will likely get some strange looks and even be dismissed as a fanatic. The power of our secularized society to deny the reality of the supernatural and the power of God is strong and growing. (Renewal is fine, as long as it is kept to a rational, manageable "program.")

And of course, the history of charismatic renewal and other forms of authentic renewal have been marked with human failure and weakness, as well as by the grace of God. So I have asked myself, "Did Sts. Benedict, Francis, Dominic, Teresa, Ignatius, and others in the Catholic tradition of renewal encounter some of the same responses and challenges as they sought to follow the Lord's call to them?"

Questions like these, from my own experience and that of the church, have led me (after many years of research and reflection) to write this book. What is authentic Catholic renewal? How does God renew his church? What can we do to promote its renewal?

We will certainly see that the paths of renewal are not always clear or easy. But no matter—we must focus on God's desire to renew his bride, the church, and continually pray:

> Come, Holy Spirit, fill the hearts of your faithful,
> And kindle in us the fire of your love;
> Send forth your Spirit, and they shall be created,
> And you shall renew the face of the earth....

CHAPTER ONE

What Is Renewal?

In the Gospel of St. Matthew, Jesus said that he would build his church upon rock and that the powers of death "shall not prevail against it" (Matthew 16:18). At the close of that Gospel, immediately before he ascended to his Father in heaven, Jesus promised his followers that he would be with them "always, to the close of the age" (Matthew 28:20). According to these promises, the church of Jesus Christ is strong and enduring. Jesus never said that at some point his followers would have to form a new church.

St. Paul spoke of the church as "the body of Christ" (1 Corinthians 12:27), and he insisted that there is "one body" (Ephesians 4:4) and that Christians always are to view themselves as united in their faith: There is "one Lord, one faith, one baptism, one God and Father of us all, who is above all and through all and in all" (Ephesians 4:5–6). St. Paul also spoke against those who caused division and factions in the church:

> I appeal to you, brethren, by the name of our Lord Jesus Christ, that all of you agree and that there be no dissensions among you, but that you be united in the same mind and the same judgment. For it has been reported to me…that there is quarrelling among you…. What I mean is that each one of you says, "I belong to Paul," or "I belong to Apollos," or "I belong to Cephas," or "I belong to Christ." Is Christ divided? (1 Corinthians 1:10–13a).

Likewise, the Acts of the Apostles twice recounts how division or threats of division of the one church were avoided or resolved (see Acts 6; 15). The New Testament understanding, therefore, is that there is and always is to be one, undivided, and universal ("catholic") church. This is confirmed by the Nicene Creed, which is both a summary and profession of Christian faith: "We believe in one, holy, catholic, and apostolic church."

Yet the New Testament also testifies that the church needs to be renewed. For example, the book of Revelation indicates that the church in Laodicea had grown "lukewarm" and was to be spewed out of the Lord's mouth (Revelation 3:14–16). This is followed by the exhortation: "Those whom I love, I reprove and chasten; so be zealous and repent. Behold, I stand at the door and knock; if any one hears my voice and opens the door, I will come in to him and eat with him, and he with me" (Revelation 3:19–20). This is a powerful image of renewal.

The book of Revelation also speaks of the church in Ephesus, which is praised for patiently enduring evil for Christ's name without growing weary. "But I have this against you, that you have abandoned the love you had at first. Remember then from what you have fallen, repent and do the works you did at first. If not, I will come to you and remove your lampstand from its place, unless you repent" (Revelation 2:4–5).

Here the Lord teaches us that a local church (the church in a particular location, as in a diocese or perhaps in a nation) can require renewal simply because it has lost its zeal, fallen away from its "first love" of God, and neglected its mission. If it doesn't repent there will be consequences: It will no longer be a light (lampstand—see Revelation 1:12–13) reflecting Christ. As Jesus said, "Let your light so shine before men, that they may see your good works and give glory to your Father who is in heaven" (Matthew 5:16). A church in need of renewal does not let the light of Christ shine clearly and brightly.

Renewal, then, is not the creation of a new church but a revitalization of the church, making her "new again" or "like new" in her practice, spirit, or ideals. The book of Revelation's idea of the church's return to its "first love" and to "the works you did at first" captures the essence of renewal. We don't need a new church, because God's plan is to renew the one church, keeping her fresh, vibrant, and fervent, as she was at her beginnings. And yet don't we often expect no more than, and settle for, a humdrum, lukewarm Christianity?

Confusion About Renewal

Many Catholics view renewal as setting a new direction for the church, rather than as a return to a love, fervor, and practice of the faith that existed previously. This view necessarily rejects old or traditional understandings and practices. The Second Vatican Council's teaching is often interpreted as this type of renewal, changing things to bring the church "up-to-date," as the Italian word *aggiornamento* is translated. This interpretation of renewal overlooks the fact that much of what the Second Vatican Council taught is an affirmation of authentic past practices and understanding of the Catholic faith. The council did implement some new things that were authentic developments of Tradition—matters of discipline or practice, not defined doctrines—as the Holy Spirit led. Overall the approach of the council was like that of the "householder who brings out of his treasure what is new and what is old" (Matthew 13:52), in order to rekindle the fervor of the church and provide new vision.

As is true with many things, discernment is needed, and in the church this is particularly the task and gift of the bishops. Ultimately they must judge what in the church ought to be renewed, reformed, or left as it is and defended.

Today the term *renewal*, as it refers to the church, often evokes a strong response—positive or negative. Often the response depends on how one perceives the overall direction of the church over the past forty or fifty years, as it has been shaped by the Second Vatican Council. Some are critical of the council, seeing it as the cause of the confusion and problems they see in the church. Others have accepted joyfully the direction set by the council, especially as it was implemented during the pontificates of Paul VI and John Paul II. Others see Vatican II as signaling the need for more change and "updating" in the church; they would like this type of renewal to continue.

For those for whom the term *renewal* has decidedly negative connotations, I propose that there is authentic renewal—the rediscovery and reappropriation of elements that truly belong to the church as it has been instituted by Jesus Christ and that therefore strengthen and enrich her. This authentic renewal unfolds in history through the power and guidance of the Holy Spirit. "By the power of the Gospel he [the Holy Spirit] permits the Church to keep the freshness of youth. Constantly he renews her and leads her to perfect union with her Spouse" (*Lumen Gentium*, 4).

Renewal and the Second Vatican Council

This last quote from the Dogmatic Constitution on the Church confirms that the Second Vatican Council was concerned with promoting the authentic renewal of the church, which is an ongoing work of the Holy Spirit. The Holy Spirit is the church's "fountain of youth," permitting the ancient church to maintain its freshness. Indeed, the very first document promulgated by Vatican II, the Constitution on the Sacred Liturgy, begins, "The sacred Council has set out to impart an ever-increasing vigor to the Christian life of the faithful" (*Sacrosanctum Concilium*, 1). This "vigor" or vibrancy is at the heart of renewal.

The Constitution on the Sacred Liturgy goes on to say that the foremost aim of the restoration and promotion of the sacred liturgy is the "full, conscious and active participation" of all the faithful (*Sacrosanctum Concilium*, 14), that the faithful may "take part fully aware of what they are doing, actively engaged in the rite and enriched by it" (*Sacrosanctum Concilium*, 11). The Eucharist itself is a renewal of the covenant between God and humanity that draws those who partake of it into the insistent love of Christ and "sets them aflame" (*Sacrosanctum Concilium*, 10).

The Second Vatican Council affirms the consistently held belief of Catholics that nothing essential is lacking in the faith, doctrine, or liturgy of the Catholic church. This is why the council states, "Every renewal of the Church essentially consists in an increase of fidelity to her own calling" (Decree on Ecumenism, 6). This renewal, as presented by Vatican II, has to do mainly with the revitalization or enlivening of the practice of the faith.

For although the Catholic church has been endowed with all divinely revealed truth and with all means of grace, yet its members fail to live by them with all the fervor that they should. As a result the radiance of the Church's face shines less brightly in the eyes of our separated brethren and of the world at large. … Every Catholic must therefore aim at Christian perfection [see James 1:4; Romans 12:1–2] and, each according to his station, play his part, that the Church…may daily be more purified and renewed, against the day when Christ will present her to himself in all her glory without spot or wrinkle [see Ephesians 5:27]. (Decree on Ecumenism, 4)

The central document of the Second Vatican Council, the Dogmatic Constitution on the Church, speaks of "Christian perfection" as the call of all Catholics to holiness, regardless of their state in life (see *Lumen Gentium*, chapter five). Holiness does not mean a certain type of pious behavior but a wholehearted response to the call and the grace first received at baptism.

Jesus himself issued the call to all people to hear his voice and to become his followers in order to find life, now and for eternity. The Gospels make it clear that Jesus did not desire a halfhearted response to his call: "You, therefore, must be perfect, as your heavenly Father is perfect" (Matthew 5:48); "He who does not take his cross and follow me is not worthy of me" (Matthew 10:38).

St. Paul wrote of himself: "I have been crucified with Christ; it is no longer I who live but Christ who lives in me; and the life I now live in the flesh I live by faith in the Son of God, who loved me and gave himself for me" (Galatians 2:20). When each of us comes to realize, as St. Paul did, that Jesus Christ loves us and died for us, we also will desire to give ourselves fully to him.

Toward the end of nearly all of St. Paul's letters, he includes an exhortation (in Greek *paranesis*, meaning "a moral exhortation") to live the gospel fully. For example, in Romans 12:9–13, he says,

> Let love be genuine; hate what is evil, hold fast to what is good; love one another with brotherly affection; outdo one another in showing honor. Never flag in zeal, be aglow with the Spirit, serve the Lord. Rejoice in your hope, be patient in tribulation, be constant in prayer. Contribute to the needs of the saints, practice hospitality.

Notice that all of these expressions of God's call to holiness require the response of the individual person, even though the call is given to the church (for example, in Laodicea) and everyone in it. A renewed church is the result of renewed individuals, people whose minds, attitudes, and lives have been transformed by Jesus Christ. As St. Paul wrote to the Christians in Corinthians, "If any one is in Christ, he is a new creation; the old has passed away, behold, the new has come" (2 Corinthians 5:17).

Renewal in Sacred Scripture
Original sin separated humanity from God. Before the coming of the Messiah, the Hebrew people cried out for deliverance from sin, and the Hebrew prophets predicted it. One of the greatest penitential psalms exclaims:

> A pure heart create for me, O God,
> put a steadfast spirit within me.
> Do not cast me away from your presence,
> nor deprive me of your holy spirit.
> Give me again the joy of your help;
> with a spirit of fervor sustain me,
> that I may teach transgressors your ways
> and sinners may return to you. (Psalm 51:10–13)[1]

The prophet Jeremiah foretells the time when the Lord "will make a new covenant with the house of Israel and the house of Judah" (Jeremiah 31:31). What will this covenant do?

> This is the covenant which I will make with the house of Israel after those days, says the LORD: I will put my law within them, and I will write it upon their hearts; and I will be their God, and they shall be my people. And no longer shall each man teach his neighbor and each his brother, saying, "Know the LORD," for they shall all know me, from the least of them to the greatest,… for I will forgive their iniquity, and I will remember their sin no more. (Jeremiah 31:33–34)

Jesus, God incarnate, is the source of renewal, the "new start," of the human race. He came and established "the new covenant in my blood" (Luke 22:20; see Matthew 26:28; Mark 14:24), "thus securing an eternal redemption" (Hebrews 9:12). Indeed, the Letter to the Hebrews describes in detail how Jesus' sacrifice of himself has made reparation for all the sins of humanity, fulfilled Jeremiah's prophecy of a new covenant (see Hebrews 10:16), and opened for us a "new and living way" to enter the sanctuary of heaven (10:20).

Yes, Jesus' mission is renewal: the renewal of the human race, through a "new covenant" with a "new commandment" ("to love one another…as I have loved you," John 13:34). It includes new power to heal, to cast out demons, and even to "speak in new tongues" (Mark 16:17). The culmination of Jesus' work at the end of time will be "a new heaven and a new earth" (Revelation 21:1) and a "new Jerusalem" (21:2). Indeed, we may summarize Jesus' work of renewal with his own words, "Behold, I make all things new!" (Revelation 21:5).

The result of the new covenant that Jesus established through his teaching, his ministry, and the shedding of his blood is the formation of a new people—the church. The church is the people who have accepted and entered into a new covenant with God through faith in Jesus and through baptism, by which people are "born anew" (John 3:3) into the life that Jesus imparts through his gift of the Holy Spirit, "the Lord and giver of life" (Nicene–Constantinopolitan Creed).

As we have seen, this new life—the renewal of the human race through the new covenant—was foretold in the Old Testament. The book of Ezekiel speaks of a time when God would gather his people from the countries where they were dispersed, bringing them back to their own land. Then God says,

> I will give them one [or "a new"] heart, and put a new spirit within them; I will take the stony heart out of their flesh and give them a heart of flesh, that they may walk in my statutes and keep my ordinances and obey them; and they shall be my people, and I will be their God. (Ezekiel 11:19, 20)

Sacred Scripture speaks of renewal in terms of giving God's people a "new heart" (a "clean heart," as in Psalm 51) and a "new spirit," which come from the sending of God's own Spirit—the Holy Spirit. As Psalm 104 declares, "When you take away their spirit, they die.... When you send forth your Spirit, they are created, and you renew the face of the earth" (Psalm 104:29, 30).

In the New Testament we see the fulfillment of the Old Testament promises with the coming of Jesus, who brings life (John 3:15, 16; 5:25–29; 6:54; 10:10; 11:25–26; 14:6) and gives the Holy Spirit lavishly on Pentecost, the birthday of the church (see Acts 2).

The Church and the Renewal of Humanity
The church itself is God's work of renewal—the renewal through Christ and the Holy Spirit of the human race according to God's plan. The Letter to the Ephesians speaks of this mystery of God's plan "to unite all things in him [Christ]" (1:10), "for through him we both [Gentiles and Jews] have access in one Spirit to the Father" (2:18). Ephesians then describes that through Christ we have been made "fellow citizens with the saints and members of the household of God, built upon the foundation of the apostles and prophets, Christ Jesus himself being the cornerstone." This church is "a holy temple in the Lord" and "a dwelling place of God in the Spirit" (Ephesians 2:19–22). It is a sign and a realization of the renewal of the human race, by which Jesus Christ has reconciled humanity with God the Father and given the human family his own life, through the shedding of his blood and the gift of the Holy Spirit.

Scripture seems to imply that the church Jesus established is a holy, even perfect society. But doesn't the church need to be renewed? The answer, of course, is yes. Even in the New Testament period, as we have seen in the book of Revelation, there is a call for renewal.

The Language of Renewal
This "newness" that God brings about through the church has been called different things by Christians: renewal, reform, revival, and restoration. What is the relationship between church renewal and church reform, revival, or restoration? The prefix *re* ("again") is a common element, but these cognates have different definitions or at least different emphases.

Revival is commonly used in the evangelical tradition for the stirring up of religious fervor, usually through preaching and prayer. Its focus is on the individual, though the goal is that the fire of renewed zeal spread to the whole congregation. Thus revival is a particular type of or approach to renewal.

Restoration is a term used by some Christians to indicate the remaking of the church when it is in severe decline or even apostasy. The goal is to recover essential Christian elements that have apparently been lost. It may be termed a radical or thorough-going reform and renewal.

Reform or *reformation* is distinct from renewal in that it stresses the correction of perceived abuses, sins, or errors that have infected the church. For example, St. Paul reproves the church in Galatia for "turning to a different gospel" (Galatians 1:6)—specifically, returning to reliance on the Jewish law to attain righteousness before God and to receive the Spirit, instead of believing in Christ (Galatians 3:1–5). St. Paul warns the church in Rome about passing judgment on others (Romans 2:1–5). He rebukes the church in Corinth about factions (1 Corinthians 3:1–9), tolerating immoral behavior (1 Corinthians 5:1–7), going to pagan courts to settle disputes (1 Corinthians 6:1–8), and competitive or improper use of spiritual gifts (1 Corinthians 14). These are instances of the need for reform—the correction of some specific error or abuse—rather than a call to renewal.

Renewal emphasizes the rediscovery and stirring up of authentic elements or aspects of the church's nature that have been neglected or forgotten, or the stirring up or revitalization of the fervor of the church in living her life and carrying out the mission Christ has given her.

Renewal of the Individual

In addition to the renewal of the church, the Scripture and Catholic tradition continually call individuals to renewal of the Christian life. For example, in the Pauline writings Christians are exhorted to "put off the old man that belongs to your former manner of life ..., and be renewed in the spirit of your minds, and put on the new man, created after the likeness of God in true righteousness and holiness" (Ephesians 4:22–24), "the new man who is being renewed in knowledge after the image of his creator" (Colossians 3:10). Paul often speaks of the renewal of the mind or a renewal in knowledge: "Do not be conformed to this world but be transformed by the renewal of your mind, that you may prove what is the will of God, what is good and acceptable and perfect" (Romans 12:2).

For St. Paul the work of Christ in each person is transformation into a "new creation" (2 Corinthians 5:17) with a new way of thinking—a "renewed mind"—that has been remade into the Creator's image and likeness. "So we do not lose heart. Though our outer man is wasting away, our inner man is being renewed every day" (2 Corinthians 4:16). This is a work of God's grace that begins in baptism (the "washing of regeneration") and culminates in eternal life. St. Paul's words to his disciple Titus summarize this:

> When the goodness and loving kindness of God our Savior appeared, he saved us, not because of deeds done by us in righteousness, but in virtue of his own mercy, by the washing of regeneration and renewal in the Holy Spirit, which he poured out upon us richly through Jesus Christ our Savior, so that we might be justified by his grace and become heirs in hope of eternal life. (Titus 3:4–7)

St. Paul exhorts his followers to seek renewal, that is, to strive to respond to God's grace. This is notable in the very personal and heartfelt words addressed to Timothy:

> But as for you, man of God,…aim at righteousness, godliness, faith, love, steadfastness, gentleness. Fight the good fight of faith; take hold of the eternal life to which you were called when you made the good confession in the presence of many witnesses. (1 Timothy 6:11–12)

> I remind you to rekindle the gift of God that is within you through the laying on of my hands; for God did not give us a spirit of timidity but a spirit of power and love and self-control. (2 Timothy 1:6–7)

Paul's message about renewal, specifically directed to individuals, is clear: You have been renewed—given a new nature—through Christ. Now you must live it, stir it up, and pursue it through Christ's grace. Nearly every Pauline letter ends with an exhortation to die to sin and to live an upright moral life in the power and strength of God.

Personal Renewal and Church Renewal

Sacred Scripture reveals God's plan for the reconciliation of the human race, especially healing the rift between God and humanity caused by sin. The Bible also speaks of this as a renewal of human nature. With the coming of Jesus Christ, each person has the opportunity to enter into, to accept, and to claim that initial renewal—"putting on" or sharing in the nature of Christ—through faith and baptism.

However, the Catholic understanding is that the work of grace begun in a person through faith and baptism needs to be renewed continually. This is done annually in the renewal of baptismal promises in the Easter liturgy. The greatest Christian feast is a fitting time for this solemn, public renewal, but why not renew one's commitment to follow the Lord and seek his grace daily in prayer?

Traditionally Catholics have prayed the Morning Offering, made acts of faith, hope, and love, and adopted other prayers as a way of renewing their commitment to follow Christ and of seeking God's grace. Pope John Paul II said that he prayed to the Holy Spirit every day, as his father had taught him to do.[2] The rosary is certainly a powerful prayer of meditation on the mysteries of Christ's life and work and of intercession. The Mass is the highest form of communal prayer. The Eucharist is a renewal of the new covenant, established by Jesus and sealed with the shedding of his blood (the "blood of the new covenant").

Why do we need these things? Because human nature, in its "fallen" condition, does not maintain commitment or focus without a constant renewal of our identity (as Christians), our allegiance (to God through Christ), and our activity (directed to extending God's kingdom and mission). A new Christian once asked his spiritual mentor why he always was praying for the Holy Spirit to be poured out on him. "Aren't you already filled with the Holy Spirit?" he asked. The mentor simply replied, "I leak."

I have been asked a similar question: "Why do you urge that we pray for the Holy Spirit to be sent to us? Haven't we already received the Holy Spirit in baptism, confirmation, and the other sacraments?" The simple answer is, "There's always more."

St. Luke often speaks of people being "*filled* with the Holy Spirit" (Acts 2:4; 4:8, 31; 9:17; 13:9; see also Ephesians 5:18), and this applies more than once to those who were first "filled" with the Holy Spirit on the Day of Pentecost: "It is not by measure that he gives the Spirit" (John 3:34). God the Father and the Son always want to give more of the Holy Spirit, and Jesus even commands his apostles to ask for this gift (see Luke 11:9–13). The account of the "little Pentecost" in Acts 4:23–31 is a powerful example of the early church experiencing a continued outpouring the Holy Spirit after Pentecost, with similar results (see Acts 4:32–37).

St. Paul had the proper perspective:

> Not that I have already obtained this [the resurrection from the dead] or am already perfect; but I press on to make it my own. Brethren, I do not consider that I have made it my own; but one thing I do, forgetting what lies behind and straining forward to what lies ahead, I press on toward the goal for the prize of the upward call of God in Christ Jesus. (Philippians 3:12–14)

Just as each Christian must advance in grace and holiness throughout life—which is ongoing personal renewal—so must the church. The church has not yet arrived at its goal of total holiness and final union with Christ. Until that time of "the renewal of all things," the church constantly needs renewal in its pilgrim journey here on earth. "The Church, to which we are all called in Christ Jesus, and in which by the grace of God we acquire holiness, will receive its perfection only in the glory of heaven, when will come the time of the renewal of all things (Acts 3:21)" (*Lumen Gentium*, 48).

And the church herself will not be renewed unless her members —all Christians—realize the need for their own renewal in Christ and earnestly seek this grace. In short, you cannot have church renewal without personal renewal. If the members of the church are not striving to be renewed in Christ, they certainly will have little or no interest in the renewal of the church.

There are those who blame or condemn the church for all her shortcomings and sins and yet see no need to amend their own lives. It is easy to blame the church for weakness or failure in Christian witness, just as it is easy to blame the government or some other group for the ills of a country. It is true that some problems become institutionalized, but even if these problems are corrected, the renewal of the church or of a nation, if it is to be of real consequence, entails its members seeking some sort of change or renewal themselves.

We will examine different models of church renewal and will discover that some renewals of the church have originated from the top, that is, through the efforts of one or a few individual leaders. But for a renewal to be sustained and truly significant, the effort and spirit must spread to many individuals.

How Is the Church Renewed?

One standard way of classifying renewal is to distinguish between renewals that are primarily initiated and carried out by the church's ordained leaders or hierarchy—renewal "from the top"—and renewal primarily initiated and carried out by other members of the church: laity, religious, and priests. The distinction is mainly between those who can effect renewal by virtue of the authority of their position or office ("top-down" renewal) and those who effect renewal mainly by virtue of a charism or charisms, particular gifts from the Holy Spirit. This latter renewal is often referred to as "grassroots renewal," because it comes forth from members of the people of God other than the hierarchy.

The hierarchy may foster grassroots renewal. St. Francis of

Assisi was a common layperson whom God used to spark a great renewal in the church, which was part of a broader renewal known as the poverty or mendicant movement. Francis' bishop and the pope did not initiate this renewal, but it would not have occurred without their recognition and encouragement of Francis' call and efforts

An important role of the Catholic hierarchy with regard to renewal movements is to discern (judge) what is truly from the Lord, encourage what is good, sometimes purifying it from imperfection, and correct or condemn that which is evil or dangerous. St. Paul summed up this task in the important oft-cited text from his earliest preserved letter, the First Letter to the Thessalonians: "Do not quench the Spirit, do not despise prophesying, but test everything; hold fast what is good, abstain from every form of evil" (1 Thessalonians 5:19–22). To his disciple Timothy he wrote: "The Lord's servant must not be quarrelsome but kindly to every one, an apt teacher, forbearing, correcting his opponents with gentleness" (2 Timothy 2:24–25). This role of discernment, guidance, and correction that belongs to the church's leaders, particularly to the bishops, became increasingly important as the history of the church unfolded.

Besides this role of discernment, church leaders promote grass-roots renewal through encouragement and through teaching that fosters renewal. For example, we could rightly call the Second Vatican Council a "council of renewal" because the teaching that issued from it fostered authentic church renewal. One of the most fundamental teachings was the call of all to holiness, inviting each person to follow actively the example and teaching of Jesus Christ, to be a saint. Only those striving for holiness will effectively renew the church.

Striving to be holy is not to be considered unusual or extraordinary but rather what being a Christian is all about. The council presented this call and challenge to every member of the church. Pope John Paul II wrote in his letter on the new millennium: "As the Council itself explained, this ideal of perfection must not be misunderstood as if it involved some kind of extraordinary existence, possible only for a few 'uncommon heroes' of holiness. The ways of holiness are many, according to the vocation of each individual" (*Novo Millennio Ineunte*, 31).

Consequently the church will be renewed by its members—laity, religious, and clergy of every "rank"—all actively striving for holiness. This means living as fully as possible the teaching of Jesus Christ, as presented by the Catholic church, in the power of the Holy Spirit. To the extent that the ordained leaders of the church teach and foster this, by word and example, they are promoting grassroots church renewal.

Ultimately church renewal depends on radical openness to God and earnestly seeking to do God's will. Jesus expressed his "formula" for renewal succinctly: "Seek first his [God's] kingdom and his righteousness, and all these things shall be yours as well" (Matthew 6:33).

Every notable renewal of the church has come about through particular individuals and groups who put God's kingdom first. It is possible for persons or movements to go astray or to break from the unity of the church while thinking that they are advancing God's kingdom. This shows the importance of humility (to submit to the judgment of the church) and discernment (to distinguish what is God's will). As the Second Vatican Council put it: "Every renewal of the Church essentially consists in an increased fidelity to her own calling" (Decree on Ecumenism, 6).

Particular Forms of Renewal

The call to holiness is the primary call of Jesus Christ to all his followers. However, there are many aspects of the mission and ministry of the church, all of which can be renewed and each of which require renewal. The Second Vatican Council's Decree on Ecumenism addressed this topic, because as the church is renewed, there is a greater opportunity for Christian unity, as the light and the face of Christ become more visible. The decree notes:

> Church renewal therefore has notable ecumenical importance. Already this renewal is taking place in various spheres of the Church's life: the biblical and liturgical movements, the preaching of the Word of God and catechetics, the apostolate of the laity, new forms of religious life and the spirituality of married life, and the Church's social teaching and activity. (Decree on Ecumenism, 6)

Each particular form of renewal is integral to the renewal of the church as a whole. As an analogy, to keep your car or truck in good repair and looking good, you occasionally must change the oil, add antifreeze and other fluids, wash it, buy new tires and wiper blades, touch up rust spots (if it's an older vehicle), and get tune-ups. Some of these things are more visible than others, some more important, but all contribute to the "renewal" of your vehicle.

The same is true of the church. The "model" we Catholics have is an "0033" (about two thousand years old), and unless it is well cared for (continually renewed), it will not function the way it should. All of its aspects—sacraments, liturgy, Christian living and morality, use of charisms, preaching, study and practice of the Word of God, priesthood, religious life, married life, lay life, relationships with Mary and the saints, communion with each other, leadership, efforts for social justice and peace, charitable works, missionary activity, prayer, and so on—need to be continually refreshed and revitalized by God through grace and the action of the Holy Spirit. All of these are parts of the church and her mission, and so they all need to be renewed at the proper time according to God's will.

An entire book, or a series of books, could be written on the development and the renewal of each of these particular aspects of the church over the course of two millennia. This book does not pretend to study thoroughly even one of these particular aspects. Rather this study hopes to discuss in more general terms what authentic church renewal is and its importance for the church, how to recognize (discern) it, and how to promote it.

I hope this book will help the reader see that every member of the church needs to be personally renewed by God's grace and needs to contribute in some way to the church's ongoing renewal. It also will examine some important historical examples of church renewal. Besides being inspirational, these will enable us to appreciate the importance of authentic church renewal as well as to recognize some of the challenges and pitfalls that can slow or divert it.

The first thing that must be established is that renewal is part of God's plan for the church. When renewal is authentic—that is, a response to God's grace carried out according to Christian principles under the guidance of the Holy Spirit—Christians always ought to be "for" it. Of course, the reality is not as simple as this. To be honest, many Catholics are satisfied with the church "the way it is" (or have no idea how it could be different or better) and hence have little or no interest in renewal. Or perhaps they have heard of or experienced inadequate or failed attempts at church renewal. Human sin and weakness prevent any renewal from being completely pure and wholly according to God's will. No individual totally comprehends God's plan nor carries it out perfectly with the wisdom, courage, and other qualities necessary for the renewal to be wholly successful (that is, according to God's perfect design).

This is why the most successful and powerful renewals of the church have been started or carried out by one or more people whom the church later recognized as saints. Truly holy people have a clearer vision or understanding of God's will than most of us, through prayer and close communion with God. They can, through their example, get people to see the need for renewal, and they have the purity of heart to promote God's plan of renewal without their own sin obscuring or obstructing it significantly. They inspire others to follow or support what they are doing, though sometimes the saint is misunderstood or persecuted initially, even by church leaders.

Hence discerning true renewal of the church and carrying it out is not easy. Like everything in the Christian life, renewal is a journey of faith, requiring virtue and perseverance. And yet it is absolutely necessary. The church cannot be the church, reflecting and communicating the life of Christ in all ways, without continual renewal. This is the teaching of the central document of the Second Vatican Council, the Dogmatic Constitution on the Church:

> The Church,...clasping sinners to her bosom, at once holy and always in need of purification, follows constantly the path of penance and renewal. (*Lumen Gentium,* 8)

In order that we might be unceasingly renewed in him [Christ] (cf. Eph 4:23), he has shared with us his Spirit who, being one and the same in head and members, gives life to, unifies and moves the whole body [of Christ]. (*Lumen Gentium, 7*)

CHAPTER TWO

The Foundation of Renewal: Repentance and Prayer

Although there are many dimensions of the church that need to be renewed, no authentic renewal takes place without repentance and prayer. Renewal is not primarily a work that we can accomplish on our own, but it is a result of and a response to God's grace. We ask God, "Send forth your Spirit, and they shall be created, and you shall renew the face of the earth."

Repentance: The First Step
One of American history's foremost figures in promoting renewal in the Protestant churches was the nineteenth-century evangelist Charles G. Finney. In his famous "Lectures on Revival," he wrote, "A revival is nothing else than a new beginning of obedience to God.... [T]he first step is a deep repentance, a breaking down of heart, a getting down into the dust before God, with deep humility, and a forsaking of sin."[1]

To repent is to acknowledge one's weakness and one's failure to live the gospel of Christ fully. Repentance requires humility—an acknowledgment that we, the church, have sinned and therefore need God's forgiveness and the grace of renewal.

If someone thinks that as individuals and as a people we Christians are fine and basically doing all that God expects of us, that person will have no interest in this book (for there is no need for renewal if everything in our lives and in the church is basically OK). Worse, though, one will have no interest in Sacred Scripture, because the Bible is replete with texts calling people to repent. Jesus is very pointed about the fact that he "came not to call the [self-] righteous, but sinners" (Matthew 9:13), that it is not the healthy that need a physician but the sick (see Matthew 9:12).

But wait, one might respond, doesn't this teaching apply to those who have not responded to Jesus' call, who are outside the community of faith? Here we could use a reality check. If we look at our own lives and the life of the church, can we claim to be sinless? It was to loyal Jews—members of God's chosen people—that Jesus said, regarding the adulterous woman, "Let him who is without sin among you be the first to throw a stone at her" (John 8:7). It was to St. Peter, who had just professed Jesus to be the Messiah, that Jesus said, "Get behind me, Satan!" (Matthew 16:23) when Peter objected to Jesus' announcement that he would suffer and die.

For Catholics, as well as other Christians, the danger of "triumphalism" lurks: It is a false pride based upon our belief that we belong to God's chosen people of the new covenant and resulting in the idea that we really don't need repentance and renewal. "I'm a good Christian/Catholic. I go to church and lead a good life. What does this talk about 'renewal' have to do with me?"

If we are honest, we know there are areas in which we need to change and to receive God's mercy and forgiveness. In some ways all of us need our lives to be renewed. As the Letter to the Hebrews reminds us, "In your struggle against sin you have not yet resisted to the point of shedding your blood" (Hebrews 12:4). We all give in to sin and need to repent and be renewed by God's grace.

The Second Vatican Council confirms these truths:

> Mother Church…exhorts her children to purification and renewal so that the sign of Christ may shine more brightly over the face of the Church. (*Lumen Gentium,* 15)

> For although the Catholic Church has been endowed with all divinely revealed truth and with all means of grace, yet its members fail to live by them with all the fervor that they should. As a result the radiance of the Church's face shines less brightly in the eyes of our separated brethren and of the world at large, and the growth of God's kingdom is retarded. Every Catholic must therefore aim at Christian perfection [see James 1:4; Romans 12:1–2] and…play his part, that the Church, which bears in her own body the humility and dying of Jesus, may daily be more purified and renewed, against the day when Christ will present her to himself in all her glory without spot or wrinkle [see Ephesians 5:27]. (Decree on Ecumenism, 4)

A Good Confession
The Catholic church has special means to enable its members to repent and be reconciled with God and neighbor: the sacrament of reconciliation or penance. A good confession not only

reconciles the individual with God and helps bring peace and order into his or her life but also "prepares the ground," so to speak, for renewal. When the value and practice of the sacrament are recognized in the church (in a parish, religious community, campus community, renewal group, or diocese), then renewal can more easily occur.

I was surprised that Charles Finney spoke at length about the need for Christians to examine their "hearts" or consciences diligently so that their repentance would be genuine and lasting. Catholics can take this as good advice in preparing for the sacrament of reconciliation.

> Fallow ground is ground which has once been tilled, but which now lies waste, and needs to be broken up and mellowed, before it is suited to receive grain.
>
> If you mean to break up the fallow ground of your hearts, you must begin by looking at your hearts: examine and note the state of your minds, and see where you are. Many never seem to think about this. They pay no attention to their own hearts, and never know whether they are doing well in religion or not; whether they are gaining ground or going back; whether they are fruitful, or lying waste. Now you must draw off your attention from other things, and look into this. Make a business of it. Do not be in a hurry. Examine thoroughly the state of your hearts, and see where you are: whether you are walking with God every day, or with the devil.
>
> Self-examination consists in looking at your lives, in considering your actions, in calling up the past, and learning its true character. Look back over your past history. Take up your individual sins one by one, and look at them. I do not mean

that you should just cast a glance at your past life, and see that it has been full of sins, and then go to God and make a sort of general confession, and ask for pardon. That is not the way. You must take them up one by one. It will be a good thing to take a pen and paper, as you go over them, and write them down as they occur to you.

Go over them as carefully as a merchant goes over his books; and as often as a sin comes before your memory, add it to the list. General confessions of sin will never do. Your sins were committed one by one; and as far as you can come at them, they ought to be reviewed and repented of one by one.[2]

Finney sees this repentance, based on a thorough examination of conscience, as the first step in the renewal of the church. Many Catholic saints have said the same thing. Finney adds two important points: First, recognizing the social nature of sin, Christians also should go to others they have offended to seek reconciliation. "A revival of religion may be expected when Christians begin to confess their sins to one another"[3] (see James 5:16). And secondly, after confessing sins, Christians need to "resolve at once, *in the strength of God, to sin no more in that way.*"[4]

I believe the importance of this cannot be overstated. There is no authentic church renewal without the pursuit of and growth in holiness of the church's members, and there is no growth in holiness without repentance from sin and heartfelt commitment to break from sin by God's grace.

Prayer for Renewal
Repentance prepares the heart to pray for renewal, without which there can be no deep and lasting renewal of the church. St. James notes that "the prayer of the righteous has great power" (James

5:16). Charles Finney believed that "[a] revival may be expected when Christians have a spirit of prayer for a revival. That is, when they pray as if their hearts were set upon it."[5] Further, "There are two...means requisite to promote a revival: the one to influence men, the other to influence God. The truth is employed to influence men, and prayer to move God."[6]

Tertullian stated that "[p]rayer is the one thing that can conquer God,"[7] while Finney explained that prayer does not change God's mind but rather produces a change in those who pray, so that God's purposes are realized in them.[8] And God's purpose— God's desire—is for the church to be renewed. So as Christians pray fervently, God's plan of renewal will be realized in the church—though always in God's way and time.

An example of the necessity of prayer and the priority of the spiritual dimension of authentic renewal may be seen in the renewal of religious life. The Second Vatican Council's Decree on the Renewal of Religious Life teaches that the "renewal of the religious life comprises both a constant return to the sources of the whole of the Christian life and to the primitive inspiration of the institutes [that is, to 'the spirit and aim of each founder'], and their adaptation to the changed conditions of our time" (*Perfectae Caritatis*, 2). However, some efforts to renew religious life after the council were so focused on external changes and adaptations to the times that prayer and the essential spiritual nature of authentic renewal were overlooked or downplayed. This approach failed to observe the final essential principle of the renewal of religious life stated in the document: "[I]t must be seriously and carefully considered that even the best contrived adaptations to the needs of our time will be of no avail unless they are animated by a spiritual renewal, which must always be assigned primary importance even in the active ministry" (*Perfectae Caritatis*, 2).

It is shocking how the number of men and women religious in the United States has declined since the time of the Second Vatican Council. One recent study reported:

> Three in four finally professed men (75 percent) and more than nine in 10 finally professed women (91 percent) [in the U.S.] are age 60 and over in 2009. There are now more women religious over age of 90 than under age 60.... In LCWR [Leadership Conference of Women Religious] institutes, fewer than 7 percent are under age 50 and less than 1 percent under age 40....
>
> Among institutes whose leaders belong to LCWR, three-fourths have either no one (32 percent) or just one or two (41 percent) in initial formation. Only a few (9 percent) have more than five.[9]

While some forms of religious life are dying out, other religious communities in the United States are attracting and retaining many new members, especially young people. The same 2009 study indicated:

> The most successful institutes in terms of attracting and retaining new members at this time are those that follow a more traditional style of religious life in which members live together in community and participate in daily Eucharist, pray the Divine Office and engage in devotional practices together. They also wear the religious habit, work together in common apostolates and are explicit about their fidelity to the church and the teaching of the magisterium. All of these

characteristics and practices are especially attractive to young
people who are entering religious life today.[10]

Is it coincidental that prayer, community life, and strong commitment to the official teaching of the Catholic church are some of
the marks of these flourishing religious communities? There is no
authentic Christian renewal without prayer and spiritual renewal
at the heart of it and as the basis for it, and neither will there be
growth of religious institutes without these. The question is, will
institutes that have diverged from centering their life in the prayer
and guidance of the church, for whatever reasons, be humble
enough to repent and to change, so that they might be renewed
and find new life and vitality?

Scriptural Teaching on Repentance and Prayer for Renewal
Sacred Scripture recounts many instances of renewal of God's
people, often in response to prayer. Many Old Testament leaders
called the Hebrew people to renew their covenant with the Lord
through prayer and sacrifice. Joshua summoned all the people to
gather at Shechem (see Joshua 24:1) and there recounted God's
mighty deeds throughout their history. He then challenged them
to choose whom they would serve and proclaimed: "As for me
and my house, we will serve the LORD" (24:15). The people
agreed: " 'The LORD our God we will serve, and his voice we will
obey.' So Joshua made a covenant with the people that day....
And Israel served the LORD all the days of Joshua, and all the days
of the elders who outlived Joshua" (24:24, 25, 31).

In this age, in which there are many competing and conflicting
voices seeking people's assent and allegiance, perhaps it would be
appropriate for the church to have a special "covenant renewal"
ceremony, in which Catholics would be called to declare their

choice to obey and serve the Lord in his church and to reject other "gods." Certainly the profession of the Creed every Sunday is a communal renewal of our faith in God, and the Eucharist is a renewal of the eternal covenant between the church and God, sealed with the blood of Jesus. Nonetheless, a special period of fasting and prayer by the whole church, followed by a solemn renewal of our covenant as a people to obey the Lord and follow his ways, could be an important occasion for the renewal of the church.

But wait, isn't this precisely what the season of Lent, culminating in Easter, is designed to accomplish? Our Catholic faith, through the liturgical year, has a biblical plan of church renewal built right into it! Do we take Lent seriously as a time of spiritual renewal?

Chapter two and the following chapters of the book of Judges portray the cycle of the history of the Jews under the judges. This cycle begins with the initial fidelity to God, followed by a falling away and lapse into sin, resulting in God's allowing his people to be punished or oppressed, leading to the people's crying out to the Lord in prayer and repenting of their sin, which finally leads to God's mercy in raising up a judge to deliver them from oppression and blessing them once again.

One of the most eloquent and powerful prayers acknowledging the goodness and greatness of God and calling for his blessing is the prayer of Solomon at the dedication of the temple (see 1 Kings 8:22–62; 2 Chronicles 6:4–42). God's response to this prayer is that, while the temple will be his dwelling place, if the king and the people eventually choose to serve and worship other gods, God will "cut off Israel from the land which I have given them.... And this house will become a heap of ruins" (1 Kings

9:7, 8). Yet, even if the king and the people turn away from God, there is still hope: "If my people who are called by my name humble themselves, and pray and seek my face, and turn from their wicked ways, then I will hear from heaven, and will forgive their sin and heal their land" (2 Chronicles 7:14). There is always the promise of forgiveness and renewal when God's people turn to him in humble prayer.

The book of Nehemiah focuses on the renewal that took place when a scroll of the book of the law of Moses was read in the assembly of the people by Ezra the priest. Ezra reminded Israel that although they had rebelled against God and were sent into exile, God was "ready to forgive, gracious and merciful, slow to anger and abounding in mercy, and did not forsake them" (Nehemiah 9:17). After confessing the sins of the people that had been revealed with the reading of God's law, Ezra and Nehemiah, the governor, wrote a document renewing their covenant with the Lord and set their seal to confirm it (Nehemiah 9:38).

The idea that is woven through these and many other Old Testament texts is that Israel repeatedly forgot God and rebelled against him, and therefore they had to turn back to God (repent) to receive his mercy and deliverance from their enemies and from the harmful, death-dealing effects of their sins. There is always hope based on the belief in God's mercy, regardless of how gravely the people have sinned. This mercy is expressed powerfully in the book of Lamentations:

> The steadfast love of the Lord never ceases,
>   his mercies never come to an end;
> they are new every morning;
>   great is your faithfulness. (Lamentations 3:22–23)

The situation of the church, God's people of the new covenant, is somewhat different in that God's mercy has been revealed fully and personally in Jesus Christ. However, it seems that the church in its quest for renewal does not understand as clearly as did Israel in Old Testament times how forgetfulness of God and failure to observe his laws result in the spread of evil and the sense of the absence of God in the world and even in the church. Renewal requires, just as much today, sincere repentance and fervent prayer for God to have mercy on us, members of the church, as well as on the world. How often are we guilty, as the prophet Haggai lamented, of busying ourselves with our own houses and affairs while the house of God "lies in ruins" (Haggai 1:9)? "How is the church to be renewed if our top priorities are our own personal affairs?" might be a present-day rephrasing of Haggai's prophecy.

And yet Haggai also speaks a word of encouragement from the Lord:

> Who is left among you that saw this house in it former glory?
> How do you see it now? Is it not in your sight as nothing? Yet
> now take courage…; take courage, all you people of the land,
> says the LORD; work, for I am with you, says the LORD of hosts,
> according to the promise that I made you when you came out
> of Egypt. My Spirit abides among you; fear not. For thus says
> the LORD of hosts: Once again, in a little while, I will shake the
> heavens and the earth and the sea and the dry land; and I will
> shake all nations, so that the treasures of all nations shall come
> in, and I will fill this house with splendor, says the LORD of
> hosts. The silver is mine, and the gold is mine, says the LORD
> of hosts. The latter splendor of this house shall be greater than

the former, says the LORD of hosts; and in this place I will give prosperity. (Haggai 2:3–9)

The "house" that God speaks of in the Old Testament is the house of Israel and the temple in Jerusalem. These, however, prefigure the fulfillment of God's plan in the new house and temple of God, the church:

> And he came and preached peace to you who were far off [Gentiles] and peace to those who were near [Jews]; for through him we both have access in one Spirit to the Father. So then you are no longer strangers and sojourners, but you are fellow citizens with the saints and members of the household of God, built upon the foundation of the apostles and prophets, Christ Jesus himself being the cornerstone, in whom the whole structure is joined together and grows into a holy temple in the Lord; in whom you also are built into it for a dwelling place of God in the Spirit. (Ephesians 2:17–22)

The treasure of this house, this temple, is neither silver nor gold (of which St. Peter said he had none—Acts 3:6) but the power and gifts of the Holy Spirit: "And his gifts were that some should be apostles, some prophets, some evangelists, some pastors and teachers, to equip the saints for the work of ministry, for building up the body of Christ, until we all attain to the unity of the faith and of the knowledge of the Son of God, to mature manhood, to the measure of the stature of the fulness of Christ" (Ephesians 4:11–13; see Romans 12:4–8; 1 Corinthians 12:4–11, 27–31, in which St. Paul identifies these and others as manifestations or gifts of the Holy Spirit).

The splendor of the church is the presence of Christ and the gifts and power of his Holy Spirit. Here the prophecy of Haggai is fulfilled: "the latter splendor of this house," the "real presence" of Jesus in the church and the indwelling of the Holy Spirit, is greater than its foreshadowing in the old covenant.

We Need to Ask

Jesus instructs, even commands, his followers to pray for the fullness of God's kingdom or rule to come (in the Lord's Prayer) and for the continual sending of the Holy Spirit. "And I tell you, Ask, and it will be given you; seek and you will find…. If you then, who are evil, know how to give good gifts to your children, how much more will the heavenly Father give the Holy Spirit to those who ask him!" (Luke 11:9, 13).

The disciples needed to ask for the Holy Spirit, the church's "living water" (John 7:38), because, as the Gospel of John explains, "as yet the Spirit had not been given, because Jesus was not yet glorified" (John 7:39). For John, Jesus' glorification is his crucifixion—his death. When the risen and glorified Jesus appeared to his followers after Easter, he told them, "Behold, I send the promise of my Father upon you; but stay in the city [Jerusalem], until you are clothed with power from on high" (Luke 24:49). "And while staying with them he charged them not to depart from Jerusalem, but to wait for the promise of the Father, which, he said, 'you heard from me, for John baptized with water, but before many days you shall be baptized with the Holy Spirit'" (Acts 1:4–5).

In response the apostles returned to Jerusalem immediately after Jesus' ascension and went to the upper room, and "all these with one accord devoted themselves to prayer, together with the women and Mary the mother of Jesus, and with his brethren" (Acts 1:14). We know the result: Pentecost, the sending of the Holy Spirit, the fulfillment of the "promise of the Father" and of Jesus. Prayer ushered in the first sending of the Holy Spirit upon the church, and prayer will precede the renewal of the church in the future.

We see this in Acts 4. When Peter and John returned from being chastised by the elders for healing a cripple in the name of Jesus, the church gathered "and lifted their voices together to God" in prayer for boldness to continue to proclaim the gospel, for the Lord to continue to "stretch out [his] hand to heal" and for "signs and wonders" to be performed in the name of Jesus (see Acts 4:24–30). What was the result of this prayer for renewed zeal and power? "And when they had prayed, the place in which they were gathered together was shaken; and they were all filled with the Holy Spirit and spoke the word of God with boldness" (Acts 4:31).

Some people have suggested that the young church portrayed in the Acts of the Apostles really didn't require renewal because its life reflected the first flowering of the life and power of the Spirit and of the risen Lord Jesus. Some important texts indicate otherwise. Acts 6 recounts a dispute in the Jerusalem church, after which seven men "full of the Spirit and of wisdom" were chosen to be the first deacons. "These they set before the apostles, and they prayed and laid their hands upon them" (Acts 6:6). When the dispute over circumcision threatened to divide the church, the elders reached a solution based on what "has seemed good to the Holy Spirit and to us" (Acts 15:28). In both of these instances, the young church faced crises that were resolved through prayer and the intervention of the Holy Spirit.

The accounts in the Acts of the Apostles also reveal the need for discussion and discernment in resolving disputes and in making good decisions. Prayer for renewal does not replace prudence and reason in setting the church's direction and in making other decisions. But for a community "rooted and grounded" in Christ through faith, prayer is necessary. And prayer is where the church always needs to begin.

Too often prayer is just a formality with which we begin and end our meetings. But Sacred Scripture teaches us that since we are seeking to serve and obey God in whatever we do, Christians need to be in deep communion with God—seeking his will and guidance and the strength and wisdom we need to carry it out. As the Letter to the Ephesians exhorts: "Pray at all times in the Spirit, with all prayer and supplication.... Keep alert with all perseverance, making supplication for all the saints" (Ephesians 6:18).

And Jesus himself told a parable about a widow and an unjust judge "to the effect that they ought always to pray and not lose heart," for "will not God vindicate his elect who call to him day and night?... I tell you, he will vindicate them speedily. Nevertheless, when the Son of man comes, will he find faith on earth?" (Luke 18:1, 7–8). If we truly believe that God can and will renew his church, we will pray.

CHAPTER THREE

Eschatological and Ecclesiological Perspectives

Renewal may be seen as a return to or a reawakening of God's plan or design for a person, a community, or the church—a "making new again," a return to fidelity to God's plan and God's covenant. In this view we look back, in a sense, to the origins of God's call and plan and seek to live out and live up to that call and plan in the present, which is only possible by God's grace and our response to that grace.

Another way of understanding renewal is to look to the future, the final goal of our journey as individuals, communities, and the church. This perspective is called eschatological, referring to *eschaton*, or the "end times," when the Lord will bring the history of the world to an end. At this point the church will be fully united to Jesus Christ, and each person who has died in the grace of Christ (possessing sanctifying grace—the grace that makes one holy) will be fully united with him in heaven, in a resurrected, glorified body.

At the Last Judgment all purification of venial sin and the effects of sin will be completed; purgatory will pass away. The plan of God will be fulfilled, "a plan for the fulness of time, to unite all things in him, things in heaven and things on earth" (Ephesians 1:10). Christ will be exalted by God the Father, who has given Jesus the name above every name (Ephesians 1:21; Philippians 2:9–11) and "has put all things under his feet and has made him the head over all things for the Church, which is his body, the fulness of him who fills all in all" (Ephesians 1:22, 23; see Colossians 1:18–20).

In terms of renewal, at that time (and not before) the church will be fully renewed. By *renewed* here we mean brought to perfection, having the fullness that God intended for his people from the beginning.

The Letter to the Ephesians speaks of this in the instruction on marriage, which is founded and modeled on Jesus' love for his bride, the church:

> Husbands, love your wives, as Christ loved the Church and gave himself up for her, that he might sanctify her, having cleansed her by the washing of water with the word, that he might present the Church to himself in splendor, without spot or wrinkle or any such thing, that she might be holy and without blemish. (Ephesians 5:25–27)

The book of Revelation describes the moment of the wedding between Christ and the "new Jerusalem," the church: "Then I saw a new heaven and a new earth…. And I saw the holy city, new Jerusalem, coming down out of heaven from God, prepared as a bride adorned for her husband" (Revelation 21:1, 2; see 21:9–14).

This eschatological perspective on renewal is important because it is based on the sure hope that the task of renewal of the church will finally succeed through the mercy and grace of God. If we only look at the present condition of our own lives, our communities (parishes, religious or lay communities, and so on), or of the church as a whole, measuring them according to the standard of the gospel, we can become discouraged. However, if we look to Jesus Christ as the one who has promised to purify and renew us and finally bring the church to perfection, then we can press on through faith and hope in Christ and his promises.

We also can give thanks to God for the saints, and especially for Mary, Mother of God, who have completed their sojourn on earth and whom the Catholic church believes are already united with God in the glory of heaven. At his death on Calvary, Christ entrusted the church, represented by John, to Mary's motherly care. So now in heaven she continues this special role of intercession for the perfection and renewal of the whole church. The example, inspiration, and intercession of Mary and all the saints are another reason for hope that the church will continue to be renewed until all its members attain the full glory of heaven.

Renewal and Ecclesiology

To understand church renewal, it is essential to have a sound understanding of the nature and theology of the church: ecclesiology. There are many dimensions of ecclesiology that are related to church renewal. The intercession of the saints and Mary for the renewal of the church is one example of this, flowing from the ecclesiological doctrine of the communion of saints.

Here I would like to explore a proposition: The church lives in a (constant) state of renewal. This means that the church is always in tension (or "caught") between what she is currently and what she is called to be—the pure, spotless bride of Christ living his gospel fully. The church has not yet attained her eschatological goal of total purity and perfection, and so she needs the grace of renewal. Vatican II speaks of this in a number of ways:

> By the power of the Gospel he [God the Father] permits the Church to keep the freshness of youth. Constantly he renews her and leads her to perfect union with her Spouse. For the Spirit and the Bride both say to Jesus the Lord: "Come!" (cf. Apoc. 22:17). (*Lumen Gentium*, 4)

> While on earth she journeys in a foreign land away from the Lord (cf. 2 Cor. 5:6), the Church sees herself as an exile. She seeks and is concerned about those things which are above, where Christ is seated at the right hand of God, where the life of the Church is hidden with Christ in God until she appears in glory with her Spouse (cf. Col. 3:1–4). (*Lumen Gentium*, 6)

> In order that we might be unceasingly renewed in him (cf. Eph. 4:23), [Christ] has shared with us his Spirit who, being one and the same in head and members, gives life to, unifies and moves the whole body. (*Lumen Gentium*, 7)

The church never can be complacent or satisfied with where she is in her journey through history to Christ. Neither can individual members of the church be complacent with where they are (or where the church is) in the journey to Christ. This does not mean we should be troubled and anxious about our own salvation or about the imperfection and failure we see in the church. These should be matters of concern but not of anxiety or despair, because we know the solution: the gift of the Holy Spirit, who unceasingly acts in the church and in our lives.

Dynamics of Renewal

It is one thing to say that the church is being constantly renewed through the action of the Holy Spirit; the next step is to examine the dynamics of renewal: how it actually happens in the church's life. This is a practical and important aspect of ecclesiology.

There are many ways that the Holy Spirit acts to renew the church. These different orientations (as I will call them) are not mutually exclusive—that is, many of them coexist and overlap in a particular renewal of the church that can be identified historically. But distinguishing these different orientations may help us understand better how God is renewing the church today.

BIBLE-ORIENTED RENEWAL

While all renewal must be biblically based (that is, following the principles revealed by God in Sacred Scripture), this approach focuses on a return to the Bible and certain key biblical principles. It focuses on faithful observance of the teaching of Sacred Scripture as a means of renewal. Here are some examples of this orientation:

- Under Nehemiah the governor and Ezra the priest, the public reading of the book of the Law prompted the Israelites to return to its faithful observance.
- St. Antony of Egypt and St. Francis of Assisi are two among many saints whose personal conversion and renewal of the church were based on hearing and obeying the word of God that they encountered in Sacred Scripture. The rule of life that St. Francis first presented to Pope Innocent III for approval was nothing more than a series of Bible quotes that he and his followers wanted to live by in a literal, radical way.

- Martin Luther initially sought to renew the church through a return to faithful observance of biblical teaching. When he broke from the Catholic church, one of his guidelines for his followers was *sola scriptura*, "Scripture alone" as the guide and authority for Christian life and for the church.

- Following Luther, many other Protestant leaders have sought the renewal of their churches and communities through "evangelical revival"—a renewal based on faithful observance of the teaching of the Bible.

- One of the key dimensions of church renewal for the Second Vatican Council was a call to regular reading and study of the Bible and living by its teaching (as well as study and living of the word of God in Sacred Tradition). This emphasis is found especially in the Dogmatic Constitution on Divine Revelation (*Dei Verbum*). Another Vatican II document urges priests to study Sacred Scripture and to proclaim it boldly in their homilies (see *Sacrosanctum Concilium* 24, 35).

SPIRITUALITY-ORIENTED RENEWAL

Renewal of the church can be fostered through a particular "spiritual way" or spirituality that attracts followers and becomes either a movement, a community, or a religious order within the church. Here we see that one way to renew the church is to focus on some aspect or aspects of the gospel. There are usually distinctive theological themes or terminologies that express the spirituality of the founder and those who follow his or her spiritual way.

Examples of this type of renewal abound in the Catholic church:

- Ignatian spirituality, flowing from the founder of the Society of Jesus (the Jesuits), St. Ignatius of Loyola. Ignatius developed a method of meditation, found in his *Spiritual Exercises*, and an approach to spiritual discernment that were instrumental in renewing the Catholic church in the sixteenth century. This spirituality has continued to be a significant source of renewal up to our own day.

- Also in the sixteenth century, St. Philip Neri and St. Francis de Sales developed spiritualities for laypeople that contributed to the renewal of the church in their time and beyond.

- Many Catholic movements and groups in the twentieth and twenty-first centuries have sought to renew the church by means of their distinctive spiritualities: Cursillo, Focolare, Opus Dei, Taize (an ecumenical community), Communion and Liberation, and others aim at a fuller living of the Christian life.

Praxis-Oriented Renewal

This is very similar to spirituality-oriented renewal and, in some cases, may not be distinguishable from it. This renewal is expressed in a unique way of living the gospel (hence *praxis*), oftentimes expressed in a rule.

- The ascetic or monastic movement was a renewal marked by a life of self-denial (asceticism) and radical social separation. The rules of these orders, such as St. Benedict's, which prescribed a balance of *ora et labora* (prayer and work), were forms that contributed in many ways to the renewal of the church, including a vibrant spiritual life.

- The poverty or mendicant movement of the twelfth and thirteenth centuries was a widespread movement promoting the practice of gospel poverty, as well as other virtues. Some branches of this movement turned heretical or schismatic, but those who remained loyal to the church, such as the

Franciscans and Dominicans, contributed significantly to the renewal of the church in their time.

- Many modern movements, such as liberation theology, focus on how the gospel is lived and see this as authentic renewal. Of course, the actions these movements advocate must be discerned.

EXPERIENCE-ORIENTED RENEWAL

This is an approach to renewal that seeks to open and direct individuals and church communities to some experience that is seen as necessary or beneficial to full Christian life. This experience may be found in biblical testimony and expressed in the form of a particular spirituality, as in the first two orientations discussed. The focus, however, is on the necessity or benefit of the experience of God or a particular form of encounter with God, either as individuals or communally. Some proponents of this type of renewal contend that it is foundational for other forms of renewal, for how can one follow Christ unless one has had a living encounter with him and (or through) the Holy Spirit?

- Perhaps the most important perennial form of "experience-oriented" renewal is found in the various forms of mysticism that have recurred in the church's life and history. It must be noted that authentic Catholic mystics do not encourage people to seek an experience of God. The focus is on seeking God through prayer, usually a deeply interior and contemplative form of prayer, which often results in an encounter with God that the teachers of mysticism attempt to explain. These teachers also seek to discern between true and false mysticism.

- Most mystics would argue that it is misleading to categorize their teaching as experience-oriented, as they would prefer to be known as prayer-oriented, God-oriented, or God-seeking renewal. Be this as it may, a common aspect of this quest for God is a perceived encounter with or experience of God or God's presence, whether it be some form of spiritual encounter or a "dark night" of the soul, which is an experience of God's apparent absence. The late medieval mystics (Richard Rolle, Walter Hilton, Dame Julian of Norwich, and others) and the great mystics of the Catholic Reformation (St. Teresa of Avila and her protégé, St. John of the Cross) are examples.

- Some evangelical Christians, who emphasize the necessity of a "born again" experience, may be termed experience oriented, although they may stress that they are first and foremost Bible oriented.

- Likewise, Pentecostal and charismatic Christians are experience oriented in that they proclaim the importance and blessing of being baptized in the Holy Spirit and of receiving (and using) the gifts of the Holy Spirit as presented and explained by St. Paul.

MISSION-ORIENTED RENEWAL

This approach to renewal seeks to enliven and implement the primary missionary mandate of Jesus: to "make disciples of all nations" (Matthew 28:19). In the history of the church her missionary fervor has waxed and waned, but God has been faithful in raising up people with zeal for proclaiming the gospel to those who have not yet heard it and to reevangelize peoples that have fallen away from authentic Christian belief and practice. Examples include those who have founded missionary orders and those who have been leaders in missionary activity or in evangelization.

SERVICE-ORIENTED RENEWAL

The church has long been marked by practical service and a wide variety of charitable works. As is true in every aspect of the church's life, these works also need to be refreshed and renewed. There are many examples of this type of renewal, such as the works of Blessed Teresa of Calcutta, St. Vincent de Paul, and St. Martin de Porres.

SOCIAL AND POLITICAL RENEWAL

Although the church is not to be identified with any particular political party or social movement, she needs constant renewal and revivification in her active promotion of justice and other social virtues. Some forms of this have been controversial, such as certain types of liberation theology. However, there is need for the continued renewal of Christ's call to be a "leaven" for the promotion of the principles and values of the kingdom of God in society and the political order. (This could also be seen as praxis-oriented renewal.)

- Christian movements and organizations that promote the values of the kingdom of God, such as civil rights, the right to life, ecology, social justice, peace, and so on could be included here, for the church is renewed when these values are actively pursued and promoted by Christians.
- *Gaudium et Spes*, the Pastoral Constitution on the Church in the Modern World of the Second Vatican Council, advanced such endeavors and thus brought about a renewal of the church in her social and political apostolate. This is also true of the papal social encyclicals, beginning with Pope Leo XIII's *Rerum Novarum* (1891), up through Pope Benedict XVI's *Caritas in Veritate* (Charity in Truth, 2009).

TRADITION-ORIENTED RENEWAL

Just as one orientation of renewal is a return to the sources of Christian life in the Bible, another type of renewal seeks to revitalize the dimension of the word of God found in Sacred Tradition. "Sacred Tradition and sacred Scripture make up a single sacred deposit of the Word of God, which is entrusted to the Church" (*Dei Verbum*, 10).

Tradition-oriented renewal is more difficult to explain and identify than some of the other forms of renewal for a couple of reasons. First, Sacred Tradition itself takes different forms, including doctrines (or dogmas) formally defined by the church; moral teaching, some of which is not formally defined but belongs to the deposit of faith because of its perennial practice by Christians; and liturgy, the official prayer of the whole church. In light of this we could identify different forms of tradition-oriented renewal as doctrinal renewal, moral renewal, and liturgical renewal.

The second reason that Tradition-oriented renewal is difficult to identify and understand is that, unlike Sacred Scripture, whose canon now is permanently determined (that is, the books of the Bible do not change), "the Tradition that comes from the apostles makes progress in the Church, with the help of the Holy Spirit. There is a growth in insight into the realities and words that are being passed on" (*Dei Verbum*, 8). Our understanding of revealed truth can deepen, as St. Vincent of Lerin (fifth century) and Venerable John Henry Newman (nineteenth century) explained, in what is sometimes referred to as the development of Christian doctrine. (Note that the magisterium or teaching office of the Church—the successors of the apostles—alone have the final authority to determine what is authentic development of doctrine, including moral teaching.)

Regarding the liturgy, it must be understood that authentic liturgical renewal is a return to the original sources of the worship of the church and a discernment of how the Holy Spirit is calling for this authentic worship to be expressed in different times and cultures. This is another form of development that must be guided by the Church's magisterium. The world's bishops at the Second Vatican Council explained this in the Constitution on the Sacred Liturgy:

> In order that the Christian people may more certainly derive an abundance of graces from the sacred liturgy, holy Mother Church desires to undertake with great care a general restoration of the liturgy itself. For the liturgy is made up of unchangeable elements divinely instituted, and of elements subject to change. These latter not only may be changed but ought to be changed with the passage of time, if they have suffered from the intrusion of anything out of harmony with the inner nature of the liturgy or have become less suitable. (*Sacrosanctum Concilium,* 21)

Accordingly, in the renewal of the liturgy undertaken by the Second Vatican Council, the bishops looked back to the ancient practice of the Christian liturgy and its development through the ages, looked to the present to determine the needs and situation of the church, and looked to the future, as the liturgy on earth is also "a foretaste of that heavenly liturgy which is celebrated in the Holy City of Jerusalem toward which we journey as pilgrims" (*Sacrosanctum Concilium*, 8).

The constitution *Sacrosanctum Concilium* sometimes refers to the council's task as the "reform" or "restoration" of the liturgy. Certainly this approach includes correction of abuses (reform) and a return to closer practice of the church's early liturgy (restoration). This was, nonetheless, a true renewal of the church in and through the liturgy, which is why the term "liturgical renewal" is appropriate. The Final Report of the Extraordinary Synod of Bishops of 1985 concluded:

> The liturgical renewal is the most visible fruit of the whole conciliar [Vatican II] effort. Even if there have been some difficulties, it has generally been received joyfully and fruitfully by the faithful. The liturgical renewal cannot be limited to ceremonies, rites, texts, etc. The active participation [in the liturgy] so happily increased after the Council does not consist only in external activity, but above all in interior and spiritual participation, in living and fruitful participation in the paschal mystery of Jesus Christ (cf. *Sacrosanctum Concilium,* 11).[1]

Bringing alive the church's life in Christ in her participation in the paschal mystery: One might say that this is the ultimate goal of all renewal!

One thing that clearly is brought to light in Tradition-oriented renewal is the important role of the church's leaders. For Catholics these would be especially the bishops and the pope, who are the preeminent pastors and teachers of the church. Changes in the liturgy, including changes for the purpose of renewal, must come finally from those authorized to make those changes: "Regulation of the sacred liturgy depends solely on the authority of the Church, that is, on the Apostolic See, and, as laws may determine, on the bishop" (*Sacrosanctum Concilium,* 22, par. 1).

Doctrine and moral teaching, the other expressions of Sacred Tradition, also are formally determined by the bishops in union with the pope. Others in the church may propose changes and seek renewal in matters of doctrine, moral teaching, and liturgy. They may even do much of the research, writing, and discussion that lead to change and renewal. Yet it is the pope with the bishops who must discern, decide, and implement changes in these areas, especially in matters that regard the universal church.

The bishops, in union with the clergy and in cooperation with religious and laity, promulgate the church's doctrinal and moral teaching and implement liturgical changes within their own dioceses and jurisdictions. In a broader sense the pope and the bishops must discern and approve all forms of renewal in the church. This is part of their responsibility, as the church's pastors, to "test everything; hold fast what is good" (1 Thessalonians 5:21).

Why do only these pastors have this authority? For the sake of unity. All should seek to discern and follow what God wants—what the Holy Spirit is "saying" and "doing"—but if the church is to advance in unity, someone must be able to determine with authority what God wants and what God is doing as it affects the church and her mission. This leads to another important topic with regard to renewal: the relationship between those who represent the church in an office, or an established leadership position, and other members of the church who wish to promote the life of the church and her renewal.

Before beginning this discussion, a final word should be said about the different orientations of renewal. The types of renewal I have discussed—oriented to renewing the church with regard to the Bible, spirituality, experience of God, Christian *praxis*, mission, social and political activity, and tradition—are not exhaustive, though I believe that most forms of church renewal can be included in these categories. We can imagine someone focusing on renewing the church as a living "community of communities" (the church as *koinonia* or "fellowship") or through ecumenical endeavors. These also may be seen as forms of renewal, though they could be considered variations or offshoots of other forms, such as spirituality-oriented renewal. The essential question is whether what is being considered reawakens some aspect of the church that has been neglected or weakened.

Charism and Institution

Earlier I proposed that the church is constantly in a state of renewal. Because the church hasn't been completely purified by the Lord and attained fullness in the glory of heaven, the members of the church cannot be satisfied or complacent. Authentic renewal is a grace of God but also a task that each member of the church is challenged to undertake in response to God's grace— the action of the renewing Holy Spirit. Hence there is a tension or "holy restlessness" experienced by those who are committed to the church and her renewal. They realize how much the church needs to be renewed in order to become that spotless bride and that fully functioning body of Christ that God desires.

There is another source of restlessness or tension in this task of renewing the church that often (perhaps even inevitably) arises in the relationship between the shepherds of the church and those who are promoting or engaged in some form of church renewal, some of whom might be pastors themselves. This reflects the tension between the perceived need to preserve the recognized, stable form of the church's life as it is lived in a particular time and place and the need that some in the church feel to respond in a new or different way to the demands of the gospel through (what they believe to be) the prompting of the Holy Spirit. These latter are fulfilling a prophetic function: They speak a particular word of God to the church for her welfare and renewal. In more traditional theological language, there is a tension between institution and charism.

This distinction is a familiar one in ecclesiology. An ecclesiology stressing the institutional aspect of the church emphasizes that Jesus founded a visible church on earth with recognized leaders (the apostles and those who succeeded them), rituals (liturgy and sacraments rooted in Jesus' own words and actions), and beliefs or doctrines expressed in prayers, creeds, and sacred writings. The institutional view of the church stresses its stability, the continuity of a way of life, and beliefs that do not change essentially over time because they are rooted in Christ, who "is the same yesterday and today and forever" (Hebrews 13:8). The guidance of the church, in this "model," is primarily from the ordained leaders, those who have received the authority to lead through their share in the priestly, prophetic, and kingly offices of Christ, which is conferred through the sacrament of holy orders. In this view the church is guided and renewed (if necessary) through the Holy Spirit, acting primarily through those leaders authorized and anointed for this task through their ordination and the specific jurisdiction assigned to them (their "canonical mission").

This institutional emphasis, it should be noted, does not (when properly understood) deny nor exclude the need for renewal in the church, though it tends to have a particular understanding of what renewal is and how it is accomplished. This understanding stresses continuity, order, and proper implementation of renewal efforts, by or under the direction of the church's ordained hierarchy. If one were to draw a diagram of how the Holy Spirit renews the church in this model, it might be a pyramid with the pope, bishops, and clergy at the top and the Holy Spirit working (down) through their ministry.

In an ecclesiology that stresses the charismatic nature of the church, the focus would be renewal from within or from the grass roots. It is based particularly upon St. Paul's theology of the gifts of the Spirit (charisms, from the Greek *charismata*, meaning "gifts"), in which every member of the church, including the hierarchy, receives gifts to be used for building up the body of Christ. These gifts, as St. Paul lists them, are very diverse, and everyone receives one or more (see 1 Corinthians 12:7). As St. Paul instructed the church in Rome:

> Having gifts that differ according to the grace given to us, let
> us use them: if prophecy, in proportion to our faith; if service,
> in our serving; he who teaches, in his teaching; he who
> exhorts, in his exhortation; he who contributes [that is, gives
> money or alms], in liberality; he who gives aid, with zeal; he
> who does acts of mercy, with cheerfulness. (Romans 12:6–8)

St. Paul lists prophecy first in this and other lists of the spiritual gifts. Prophecy is important because it enables the church to understand what God desires to speak to it now for its growth, guidance, and renewal. The emphasis of the charismatic dimension of the church is prophetic, seeking to respond to God's word and direction as it is heard and appropriated in the present time.

All members of the church actively contribute to the service, upbuilding, and renewal of the church in their own particular way through the use of their gifts and their response to the guidance and promptings of the Holy Spirit they receive. If a diagram of this understanding of the church were drawn, it might be either a circle, with Christ at the center and all the members gathered around him, or a pyramid, with the Holy Spirit, who like the wind "blows where it wills" (John 3:8), inspiring action in people of every rank, from the top (the hierarchy) to the bottom (the laity). This ecclesiology is expressed in the Dogmatic Constitution on the Church:

> It is not only through the sacraments and the ministrations of the Church that the Holy Spirit makes holy the People, leads them and enriches them with his virtues. Allotting his gifts according as he wills (cf. 1 Cor. 12:11), he also distributes special graces among the faithful of every rank. By these gifts he makes fit and ready to undertake various tasks and offices for the renewal and building up of the Church, as it is written, "the manifestation of the Spirit is given to everyone for profit" (1Cor. 12:7). Whether these charisms be very remarkable or more simple and widely diffused, they are to be received with thanksgiving and consolation since they are fitting and useful for the needs of the Church. (*Lumen Gentium,* 12)

In reviewing these two approaches to renewal, it becomes apparent that both of them are biblical and Catholic. (The institutional model is fully documented in chapter three of *Lumen Gentium.*) Two further conclusions may be drawn:

1. The institutional and charismatic ecclesiologies are complementary, not conflicting.
2. Yet there is a dynamic tension that exists between them in the actual process of the church's renewal—that is, a dynamic tension exists between those responsible for testing and guiding renewal according to the nature and needs of the church, and

those who seek renewal and strive for it prophetically through the use of their charisms. Both ecclesiologies are necessary, reflecting the fact that Christ has established the church with a permanent structure and nature, and yet the church must always be renewed and open to the freely given gifts and prophetic guidance of the Holy Spirit.

Working Together to Renew the Church

First let's explore the complementarity of these two theological approaches. Beginning in the mid–twentieth century, a great deal of attention has been given to this topic in the Catholic church. One who is serious about this subject must study the writings of Karl Rahner, Hans Urs von Balthasar, Yves Congar, and Avery Dulles, to name but a few of the most prominent Catholic theologians who have addressed this topic.

In terms of the Catholic magisterium, Pope Pius XII addressed the issue in his 1943 encyclical letter on the Mystical Body of Christ (*Mystici Corporis Christi*). He asserts that both the charismatic and the hierarchical (institutional) dimensions of the church "derive from the same divine source," and he "condemns the view that the structure (*structuram*) of the Church consists solely of hierarchical elements and not of charismatic elements as well."[2]

At the Second Vatican Council, the topic arose in the discussion of *Lumen Gentium*. In a famous council speech, Cardinal Leon-Josef Suenens challenged the opinion that charisms existed primarily in the primitive church and were "nothing more than a peripheral and unessential phenomenon in the life of the Church." He recalled that, according to St. Paul, the church must be seen "as a living web of gifts, of charisms, of ministries," and that "each and every Christian, whether lettered or unlettered, has his charism in his daily life."[3] The result was the inclusion of statements about the charismatic dimension of the church in *Lumen Gentium* 4, 7, and 12, as well as in the Decree on the Apostolate of the Laity 3. Besides the charisms of the nonordained, bishops have the "sure charism of truth" (*Dei Verbum*, 8), and the church possesses the charism of infallibility (see *Lumen Gentium*, 25).[4]

Since this council the popes have continued to teach that the charismatic and institutional dimensions of the church are complementary. Pope Paul VI, on May 25, 1973, declared that the Holy Spirit brings about accord "between the charismatic inspiration and juridical structure of the Church."[5] Pope John Paul II taught on this theme on a number of occasions. On June 24, 1992, he reflected on *Lumen Gentium* 12:

> [T]he development of the ecclesial community does not depend only on the institution of ministries and sacraments, but is also furthered by the free and unforeseeable gifts [charisms] of the Spirit, who works outside established channels, too. Because of this bestowal of special graces it is apparent that the universal priesthood of the ecclesial community is led by the Spirit with a sovereign freedom ("as he wishes," St. Paul says [1 Cor 12:11]) that is often amazing.

Although the Spirit works freely through the charisms, Pope John Paul II, in the same address, presented some "criteria of discernment" that can be applied by "ecclesiastical authority or by spiritual masters and directors" to verify that the charisms are being used properly within the institutional order of the church. They are

> *Agreement with the Church's faith in Jesus Christ* (cf. 1 Cor. 12:3)....

> *The presence of the "fruit of the Spirit: love, joy, peace"* (Gal 5:22)....
>
> *Conformity with the Church's authority* and acceptance of its directives...(1 Cor. 14:37). The authentic charismatic is recognized by his sincere docility to the Pastors of the Church.... A charism cannot cause rebellion or a rupture of unity....
>
> *The use of charisms* in the community is subject to a simple rule: "Everything should be done for building up" (1 Cor. 14:26), i.e., charisms are accepted to the extent that they make a constructive contribution to the life of the community, a life of union with God and of fraternal communion. St. Paul insists firmly on this rule (1 Cor 14:4–5, 12, 18–19, 26–32).[6]

Even here we can glimpse the inherent tension between the charismatic and institutional. The Spirit moves a person with sovereign freedom "as he wills," and yet one must be docile and obedient to the pastors of the church. All is well—as long as the charisms are recognized, appreciated, and understood by the pastors, and the recipient of a charism or a leading of the Holy Spirit remains docile and obedient to the pastors, even when the charism or leading is not accepted or appreciated. Of course, Pope John Paul's teaching is wise and totally biblical, but its promulgation and implementation remain a challenge.

A Wealth of Gifts

In 1994 Pope John Paul II reminded the laity that, according to Vatican II, "From these charisms there arises 'for each of the faithful the right and duty of exercising them for the good of men and for building up the Church' (*Apostolicam Actuositatem*, 3)." He noted that the council has changed our way of thinking about the charisms listed by St. Paul, "such as healings, the gift of prophecy or that of tongues," from being "extraordinary" to "*gifts* belonging to the *ordinary* life of the Church."

> We cannot but admire the great wealth of gifts bestowed by the Holy Spirit on lay people as members of the Church in our age.... At the beginning of the Christian era extraordinary things were accomplished under the influence of charisms.... This has always been the case in the Church and so in our era as well.

He also repeated that "no charism dispenses a person from reference and submission to the Pastors of the Church" (*Christifideles Laici*, 24).[7]

Pentecost 1998 was a landmark event in Pope John Paul II's pontificate. He invited members of all the ecclesial movements and predominantly lay communities to celebrate Pentecost with him in Rome. Over half a million of them showed up, one of the largest (if not the largest) convocations at the Vatican in history. At this gathering Pope John Paul II said that "[t]he institutional and charismatic aspects are co-essential, as it were, to the Church's constitution."[8]

Two months later, in his general audience of August 5, 1998, the pope said:

> In accordance with the message of Paul..., often recalled and illustrated by the Second Vatican Council (cf. *Lumen Gentium*, n. 12), there is no such thing as one Church according to a "charismatic model" and another according to an "institutional model."...[O]pposition between charism and institution is "extremely harmful."[9]

Finally John Paul II wrote on the Jubilee of the Apostolate of the Laity (November 21, 2000):

The Church is a mystery of communion which originates in the life of the Blessed Trinity. She is the Mystical Body of Christ. She is the People of God who, made one by the same faith, hope and charity, journey through history to their definitive homeland in heaven. And we, as the baptized, are living members of this marvelous and fascinating organism, nourished by the sacramental, hierarchical and charismatic gifts which are coessential to it. That is why, today more than ever, it is necessary for Christians, enlightened and guided by faith, to know the Church as she is in all her beauty and holiness, so that they can listen to her and love her as their mother.[10]

Open to the Spirit

Pope Benedict XVI has reiterated this teaching in his pontificate. In his *Regina Coeli* address on Pentecost 2005, he called attention to "the indissoluble bond that exists in the Church between the Spirit and the institution."

> Without the Holy Spirit, the Church would be reduced to merely a human organization, weighed down by its own structures…. Christ, who established the Church on the foundation of the Apostles closely around Peter, has also given it the gift of his Spirit, so that throughout the centuries he would be the comfort (cf. Jn 14:16) and the guide to the entire truth (cf. Jn 16:13). May the Ecclesial Community remain always open and docile to the action of the Holy Spirit, to be among men and women a credible sign and efficacious instrument of God's action![11]

In 2006 Pope Benedict followed the example of Pope John Paul II in inviting all the new movements and ecclesial communities to Rome to celebrate Pentecost. On Pentecost Eve, June 2, 2006, the patriarch of Venice, Cardinal Angelo Scola, gave an address in which he explained "co-essentiality": the fact that the institutional and charismatic dimensions of the church are not two separate components from which the church arises but rather express a dual unity proper to the church. That is, every action carried out by the church is both institutional and charismatic. Further, he said, it is a mistake to relegate movements to the charismatic dimension of the church, and dioceses, parishes, and traditional groups to the institutional. Both of these dimensions belong to each and every Catholic group.[12]

The following day Pope Benedict emphasized three works of the Holy Spirit: life, freedom, and unity. Toward the conclusion of his talk, he exhorted:

> May you take part in the edification of the one body. Pastors must be careful not to extinguish the Spirit (cf. 1 Thes 5:19) and you will not cease to bring your gifts to the entire community. Once again, the Spirit blows where he wills. But his will is unity. He leads us towards Christ through his Body.[13]

In an address to members of Communion and Liberation on March 24, 2007, Pope Benedict made absolutely clear his agreement with Pope John Paul II regarding the complementarity of the charismatic and institutional aspects of the church:

> In the Message to the World Congress of Ecclesial Movements, 27 May 1998, the Servant of God John Paul II had this to say: that there is no conflict or opposition in the Church between the institutional and the charismatic dimensions, of which the Movements are a significant expression. Both are co-essential

to the divine constitution of the People of God. In the Church the essential institutions are also charismatic and indeed the charisms must, in one way or another, be institutionalized to have coherency and continuity. Hence, both dimensions originate from the same Holy Spirit for the same Body of Christ, and together they concur to make present the mystery and the salvific work of Christ in the world.

This explains the attention with which the Pope and the Pastors look upon the richness of the charismatic gifts in the contemporary age.[14]

Here Pope Benedict alludes to how the charismatic and institutional dimensions of the church are complementary. On the one hand the structural or institutional aspect of the church, by which we especially mean the ordained offices of leadership and service, is based on both the grace conferred by the sacrament of holy orders and the particular charisms that the Holy Spirit has given to qualify and equip that person to carry out the office successfully (for example, charisms of teaching, pastoring, discernment, healing, and so on). Put simply, the church's hierarchy is charismatic.

God gives the charisms to build up the institution of the church. And the charisms need to be guided and ordered ("institutionalized") so that they can serve the community of the church, with all its members working together cooperatively.

A Dynamic Tension

Now that we've seen that the institutional and charismatic ecclesiologies are complementary and not conflicting, let's consider the second conclusion: that there exists a dynamic tension between the institutional and the charismatic dimensions of the church in the actual process of renewal. That is, in the life of the church, renewal is not something that always occurs smoothly or easily. This can happen because the church's members refuse to repent and pray, because they fail to acknowledge or even recognize that the church needs to be renewed, or because they do not recognize the role of the pastors of the church to discern and guide renewal. The church's renewal can be slowed or obstructed if pastors and proponents of renewal do not see eye-to-eye.

Even when there is good will and openness to the Holy Spirit on both sides, tension can and often does arise. Pastors and other church members may not see the need for a particular type of renewal or an approach to renewal that some people want. Those who are calling for renewal or for the recognition of their charisms may not understand the reservations that pastors have about what they propose or about the use of their gifts. Pastors and others may think that these "prophetic" folks are pushy or insubordinate, while proponents of renewal may think that the others (including pastors) are complacent or are "stifling the Spirit" (see 1 Thessalonians 5:19).

On this theme Karl Rahner wrote an essay entitled "Do Not Stifle the Spirit!" First he notes that "we should tremble" at the possibility that humans could stifle the Spirit of God, and yet, as Jesus humbled himself in subjecting himself to humanity, so has the Holy Spirit.[15] There is always the danger of forgetting that it is God who directs the church through the Holy Spirit. Both those in authority in the church and those who are given other charisms must be obedient to the Spirit of God. Rahner wrote:

> The spirit of true obedience is present not so much where the
> official machinery of the Church is running smoothly and

without friction...but rather where the non-official movements of the Spirit are recognized and respected by the official
Church in the context of a universal striving for the will of
God, while the "charismatics" for their part, while remaining
faithful to their task, maintain an attitude of obedience and
respect towards the official Church. For it is God and God
alone who builds the one Church, shaping the true course of
her history as he himself wills out of the materials of the mul-
tiplicity of spirits, tasks and ministries in the Church, and out
of the ensuing tensions and oppositions which are so necessary. And further this course may seem quite different from the
one thought out and planned in the official councils of the
Church's ministers, even though those are quite right and are
only fulfilling their bounden duty in so planning a course for
the Church.[16]

This tension between the institutional and charismatic dimensions of the church can turn out to be either destructive and divisive or positive—what may be called "dynamic tension." The tension can be destructive if it results in factions, scandal, suspicion,
and the like. Sometimes this occurs at the outset of an attempt at
renewal, when what is happening is perceived as a conflict, a misunderstanding that leads to polarization ("us vs. them" language
or thinking) and finally to division of some sort. The idea of the
church as a mystery of communion is not realized.

On the other hand, the tension in the call for renewal and in
the interaction between the institutional and charismatic dimensions of the church can be constructive and lead to the purification and growth of all. For this to happen, charity must prevail.
There must be a willingness to think the best about the goals and

motives of others in the church and to act accordingly. There must be an honest effort to understand other points of view and to be reconciled and forgiving if hurtful differences arise.

St. Paul, in his instruction on the use of the charisms, said, "Make love your aim, and earnestly desire the spiritual gifts, especially that you may prophesy" (1 Corinthians 14:1). Prophecy is not normally predicting the future but speaking the word that God wishes to communicate in a given moment and situation. When a prophetic message is delivered and heeded, the future unfolds according to God's will, and the words of the Lord's Prayer are realized: "Your kingdom come, your will be done on earth as it is in heaven."

Authentic church renewal is normally initiated by a prophetic sense, or "word," that God desires something to happen. When this message is brought to the church by one who is exercising this charism, it can be (and usually is) challenging, just as Jesus' teaching is challenging to those who really hear it and desire to respond to it. This is one reason why there may be tension between the institutional dimension of the church, which may seek to preserve stability and order, and the charismatic dimension when it plays this prophetic role, calling for change and renewal.

Yet in this tension God directs the church and enables it to grow in virtue, which it will if all members seek to act in charity and to be open to the Holy Spirit's work. It is also important for all to remember that the action of the Holy Spirit is a gift to be received—not something anyone in the church can control (which would only "stifle the Spirit"). Thus renewal that is a work of the Holy Spirit is a prophetic action, often challenging the way we live, think, speak, and act, with the "sword" of God's truth, his word (see Ephesians 6:17).

Renewal is often not comfortable but challenging, and hence it causes conflict. "Speaking the truth in love" (Ephesians 4:15) is constructive if approached the right way. The late Cardinal Avery Dulles wrote some years ago:

> Ideally the institutional and the charismatic, since they proceed from the same Lord and are intended for the same goal (the edification of the Church in love), should be responsive to each other. Correction from either side, where needed, should be humbly accepted by the other in a spirit of gratitude and conciliation. But as Church history abundantly attests, clashes occur in which each side is convinced that it cannot yield without compromising on a matter of principle. Such clashes, always painful, sometimes lead to the brink of schism, and beyond. Are there rules for resolving these conflicts?
>
> It is often said that the last word lies with the office-holders, since it is their function to discern between true and false charisms—a point made more than once in the *Constitution on the Church*. The presumption does lie with the hierarchy, but the presumption cannot be absolutized. Rahner wisely remarks: "Provision has to be made that bureaucratic routine, turning means into ends in themselves, rule for the sake of rule and not for the sake of service, the deadwood of tradition, proud and anxious barricades thrown up against new tasks and requirements, and other such dangers, do not extinguish the Spirit." Thus there is no ultimate juridical solution to collisions between spiritually gifted reformers and conscientious defenders of the accepted order. The Church is not a totalitarian system in which disagreement can be ended by simple fiat. Rather, it is an open society in which all parties are subject to correction. All must recognize their limitations and treat the others with patience, respect, and charity.

> In a pilgrim Church time is needed to sift the good grain
> from the chaff, the weeds from the cockle (cf. Mt 13:24–30,
> 36–43). If a true consensus is to be achieved, it must be the
> work of the Spirit, who dwells not in the hierarchy alone but
> in all the faithful, as we are taught by Vatican II. In this sense,
> charism has the last word. To quote Rahner again: "The har-
> mony between the two 'structures' of the Church, the institu-
> tional and the charismatic, can only be guaranteed by the one
> Lord of both, and by him alone, that is to say, charismati-
> cally."[17]

Our study of renewal in church history will illustrate how
renewal has emerged charismatically and how it has been discerned and guided by the church's hierarchy.

We have seen, then, that the institution of the church is funda-
mentally rooted in her hierarchical structure. Members of the
hierarchy receive their office through a divine call and through
charisms that are given freely by the Holy Spirit but that also are
conferred and strengthened through the sacrament of holy
orders.[18] Thus the hierarchy of the church is founded both on
charisms and on the sacraments. The institution of the church is
charismatic in its essence as well as sacramental.

Conclusions

What can we conclude about church renewal from the perspectives of ecclesiology and eschatology?

First, it is God, the sovereign Lord of the church, who plans and
directs its renewal. True renewal of the church is a work of the
Holy Spirit, who uses many different human agents according to
their unique calls and gifts (charisms). One of the tasks of those
called and gifted to lead the church—the ordained hierarchy—is

to discern various gifts of those in the body of Christ in order not to "quench [or stifle] the Spirit" nor to "despise prophesying" but to "test everything" and to "hold fast to what is good," as St. Paul said so simply and directly (1 Thessalonians 5:19–21).

In some instances church leaders may have to correct or redirect activities that they judge are not works of the Spirit or are not being carried out properly, for the good of the whole church. In others they may simply need to make room for those gifts and activities that are from the Holy Spirit—in short, to get out of the way and let God act!

The job of those whom God is using to renew the church (which includes those who belong to the hierarchy) is to be faithful to the call and action of the Holy Spirit and to be obedient to those in authority, through whom the Holy Spirit also acts. Those in authority must avoid the temptation to dominate or control the gifts of God, following their own preconceived agendas and plans. Those who have received gifts for the church's renewal must not get "swelled heads" (pride) because God is using them (or the groups or movements to which they belong) to renew the church. Humility is always needed. Recall that God was able to speak through a donkey (see Numbers 22:28)!

John the Baptist rebuked the pride of the Pharisees and Sadducees, reminding them that even though they were children of Abraham, they had to repent and humble themselves, for "God is able from these stones to raise up children to Abraham" (Matthew 3:9). As Jesus taught us: "So you also, when you have done all that is commanded you, say, 'We are unworthy servants; we have only done what was our duty'" (Luke 17:10).

A correct and full understanding of the theology of the church in this area can help everyone work together to advance God's plan of ongoing renewal. We recall, from the eschatological perspective, that the Lord must continue to purify and renew the church to prepare her for his final coming. It is easy to become frustrated or discouraged when we encounter trials and difficulties in this process. Those seeking renewal may become impatient or frustrated with members of the hierarchy and with other Catholics who appear resistant to renewal or do not understand it. Those responsible for pastoring the church may not want to deal with the challenges and conflicts that renewal entails. Or they may fear not supporting the prophetic word that the Lord desires the church to hear. Everyone is challenged to pray earnestly to know God's will and to have the courage to respond to it, so that the kingdom of God will be revealed and come more fully "on earth as it is in heaven."

It is possible to place too much emphasis on the conflicts, difficulties, and challenges of renewal. The renewal of the church is, in the end, powerful, positive, and life-giving. It brings new spiritual life and vibrancy to the church, making her shine more brightly with the radiance of Christ. Consider the joy of the meeting of Pope John Paul II at the Vatican with the half million representatives of new ecclesial movements and communities at Pentecost 1998! The experience of renewal demonstrates that the church is alive with Jesus' presence and power, giving hope and assurance that his bride is truly being prepared for his final coming.

Yes, renewal is not easy, but is there anything good in life, like a happy marriage and family life, that doesn't have the cost of some struggle to achieve and maintain?

In 1998 Cardinal Joseph Ratzinger pointed out that the best way to understand renewal is not by analyzing the institutional and the charismatic, or the Christological and the pneumatolog-ical, or the structure and the prophetic dimensions of the church, but rather by looking at the unfolding of the church's history in which God acts.[19] In the next two chapters we will explore some important historical examples of church renewal.

CHAPTER FOUR

The Power of Personal Charism

Over the course of twenty centuries, waves of renewal have continually swept through the Church, for as the poet T.S. Eliot wrote:

> And the Church must be forever building, . . . and always being restored. . . .
>
> . . . [F]or it is forever decaying within and attacked from without.[1]

The impulse for renewal is very often actualized by an individual or group who respond to God's grace. If the renewal is authentic —from God—then it is sparked and carried out by means of the gifts of the Holy Spirit that the person or group possess and use for the building up of the church. The leaders of renewal groups may be charismatic in the Weberian (sociological) sense of being dynamic and appealing, but this is not necessary, since true renewal is based on God's power and grace and not on human personality.

The title of this chapter, "The Power of Personal Charism," must be understood in this light. *Charism* means "a gift of the Holy Spirit," and *personal* refers to being "granted to a person" for the building up of the body of Christ, not for one's own personal benefit (see Romans 12:6–8; 1 Corinthians 12:7; 14:5, 12, 26; Ephesians 4:8, 11–13).

Throughout the church's history God's power through personal charism has been manifested in many ways: in evangelization and missionary activity, in care for those in need, in confronting injustice courageously, and so on. Here we will focus on individuals and groups whose charisms and activities led to or contributed to the renewal of the church.

Also in this chapter we will focus on agents of renewal who were not bishops or popes and thus did not have the authority of an ecclesiastical office to promote or institute church renewal. We will also consider here cases of personal charism that either failed in the quest for renewal or resulted in division of the church (schism) or doctrinal error (heresy). Not all heretical individuals or groups will be considered but only some who were seeking to renew the church and ended in doctrinal error or schism.

When informed Catholics make an impromptu "short list" of important figures in the church's history of renewal, certain names invariably appear. Karl Rahner wrote: "Anthony the Hermit, Benedict, Francis of Assisi, Catherine of Siena, Margaret Mary Alacoque, Theresa of the Child Jesus and many others have all been of irreplaceable importance for the history of the Church …in their function of direct receptors of the impulses of the Spirit."[2]

Father Avery Dulles wrote: "The founders of great movements of reform, such as Francis of Assisi, Ignatius of Loyola, and Teresa of Avila, have been loyal servants of the institution. Generally speaking, the more deeply a prophet or reformer is immersed in the heritage [of the Church], the more successfully will he or she be able to transform and renew it with fidelity to its authentic spirit."[3]

Pope John Paul II, speaking of the renewal of spirituality, attests to the importance of the "giants" of the Catholic mystical tradition: "How can we forget here, among the many shining examples, the teachings of St. John of the Cross and St. Teresa of Avila?" He says this in the context of urging that "our Christian communities must become genuine 'schools' of prayer" (Novo Millennio Ineunte, 33).

Pope Benedict XVI, in his address to the ecclesial movements, spoke of the contributions of renewal figures who did not belong to the church's hierarchy: St. Antony of Egypt, St. Francis of Assisi, St. Basil of Caesarea (before he was made a bishop), St. Dominic Guzman, St. Hildegard of Bingen, St. Catherine of Siena, Mary Ward, and St. Teresa of Avila.[4]

None of these authors were seeking to produce a complete list of important figures in the church's renewal, and others were named in passing as well. What should interest us is that many of the same names recur. These certainly must be figures who should be studied to understand how God acts through personal charism to renew the church.

Without attempting here to produce an exhaustive history of renewal, it may help to understand how God acts to renew the church by studying just a few of these key figures and their history. As the bishops of the Extraordinary Synod of 1985 wrote:

"Men and women saints have always been founts and origins of renewal in the most difficult circumstances throughout the Church's history. Today we have tremendous need of saints, for whom we must assiduously implore God."[5]

The Early Church
Primitive and early Christianity is replete with martyrs and other saints who were the "living stones" upon which Christ's church was built (see 1 Peter 2:5; Ephesians 2:19, 20) and who inspired Christians of their own day and for generations to come. The church of this period stands as a model in its witness and vibrancy, even though it was imperfect and still developing in its structures, doctrine, and other aspects of its self-understanding. Many Christians have looked back to this period, longing for a restoration of the "honeymoon" period of the church, when all was fresh in the grace of Pentecost.

Sadly, one of the first of those clearly calling for renewal was Montanus, a priest of a town in Phrygia (in present-day Turkey) in the mid- to late second century. Montanus bemoaned the lack of spiritual fervor and the gradual disappearance of the Pauline charisms, especially prophecy. In response he established an extended period of fasting (two additional weeks before Lent) and encouraged the use of the spiritual gifts. He delivered prophetic messages and propagated the prophecies of others in his congregation, such as those of two prophetesses, Priscilla and Maximilla. The movement was known as the New Prophecy.

Soon the news of this incipient renewal spread into other parts of Phrygia and beyond, leading to meetings (synods) of concerned bishops in areas affected by "Montanist" teaching and prophecy. Christians were attracted by the call for a more fervent practice of the faith and longed for prophetic words. However, the bishops thought that Montanus and his followers were viewing themselves as true "spiritual" members of the church, while those who did not follow their practices or heed their prophecies were lax or "carnal" Christians. Some bishops probably misunderstood the form of prophetic speech Montanus employed and considered him a heretic posing as the Holy Spirit. The bishops decided to restrict the activities and prophecies of Montanus and his followers, claiming they were questionable and potentially divisive.

It is important to note that the bishops of Phrygia never outrightly condemned the use of the charisms but only insisted that these gifts of the Spirit be submitted to the discernment of the bishops and that they not be considered normative or necessary for the whole church. Tragically, Montanus rejected the directives of the bishops, and the movement separated from the universal church—one of the first schismatic churches (or "anti-churches") and the first division over a matter of practice or discipline, not doctrine.

The Montanist movement might have died out quickly after its condemnation were it not for the prominence of the group's greatest theologian, the North African convert and Christian apologist Tertullian of Carthage. His influential writings, after he became a Montanist at the beginning of the third century, kept the movement alive, drew much attention to it, and won new adherents. After his death Montanism began to decline.

Montanism undermined the future renewal of the church by casting doubt on the validity of any group that advocated stricter penitential practices, the use of charisms (especially prophecy), and even the idea of renewal of the church. Suspicions emerged and persisted that such groups were not really in the mainstream of the church. This reaction against the extremes and abuses of the Montanists threatened to make the church narrower, quenching the zeal for holiness and her charismatic heritage. We recall St. Paul's warning against "quenching" or stifling the Spirit. And St. Peter wrote, "Prophecy has never been put forward by man's willing it. It is rather that men impelled by the Holy Spirit have spoken under God's influence" (2 Peter 1:21). There was a danger that authentic prophecy would not be welcomed in the church due to its association with Montanism and its errors.

Montanism also reminds us of the fact that influential leaders of movements have the potential to do the church tremendous good or tremendous harm, depending on how they use their gifts and the choices they make with regard to church authority.

Monasticism

Fortunately, a movement arose at the end of the third century that held many of the same ideals as Montanism but approached the church in a different way. As a result it won widespread ecclesiastical approval and renewed the church profoundly. This movement, called monasticism or the ascetic movement, was the most powerful source of authentic renewal in early Christianity.

In order to appreciate the timeliness and influence of asceticism, it is necessary to understand the era in which it emerged. Constantine became emperor toward the beginning of the fourth century, and Christianity was legalized through the Edict of Milan in AD 313. As a result the martyrdom of Christians ceased, and many people flocked to join the church, as it was now safe and in some places politically and socially advantageous. The major negative effect was a loss of fervor, now that being a Christian was no longer countercultural nor life-endangering.

There were those who had the vision and the zeal to create a new Christian culture to replace or transform the Greco-Roman culture of the Empire. The monastic or ascetic movement fostered a radical living of Christianity that was certainly zealous but focused on attaining holiness through a physical separation if its adherents from the world as well as a renunciation of the normal, everyday life and activities of society. How could such a movement, which sought to renounce the world, transform the world?

The amazing thing is that monasticism did contribute both to the renewal of the church and to a transformation of society, though the latter could be viewed as a process that unfolded over the course of centuries. This powerful work of renewal began with individuals who simply wanted to respond personally to the words of Jesus, "If you would be perfect, go, sell what you possess and give to the poor, and you will have treasure in heaven; and come, follow me" (Matthew 19:21).

There were probably many who responded to that call, but the one who is known as the father of monasticism is Antony of Egypt. St. Athanasius, bishop of Alexandria, was Antony's "publicist," spreading knowledge of the monastic movement through his *Life of Antony*. Years after this biography was written in Egypt, it contributed to the conversion of St. Augustine, who had heard about it in Milan. After he was baptized, Augustine lived an austere, monastic life with some friends—a community of philosophers—and after he became a bishop, he organized the priests in his diocese into a quasi-monastic community in service to the church, for which he wrote a famous rule of life. One author notes that "some thirty male monasteries inspired by the Augustinian experience...still exist to this day in North Africa."[6]

It is noteworthy that Antony began his life of penance and solitude before Constantine came to power—when Christians were still being persecuted for belonging to an illegal religion. Antony was truly a prophetic figure in calling the church to a deeper life of prayer, penance, and self-denial. This was important during the persecution of Christians but would be even more important when persecution ceased and the fervor of the church needed to be rekindled. God, the author of all renewal, was unfolding his plan.

Antony's radical response to God's Word became a fire that spread among Christians, first in Egypt (his home) and then in Syria, Asia Minor, and eventually throughout the Empire. Christians who did not separate themselves from the world were either inspired, challenged, or convicted by the stories of the ascetics' penitential lives or by the sayings of the desert fathers that were propagated by pilgrims and the curious. There were no longer martyrs, but in the ascetics the church found new icons of renewed Christian life. These ascetics were, when they lived together guided by a rule, the first religious orders and communities. As one author described it:

> The experience of monasticism would reinvigorate the somewhat enfeebled life of Christians. It would give renewed vigor to the life of the Church; help shape the liturgy; promote the development of new forms of ministerial life and new forms of spirituality among the faithful; encourage the growth of ecclesial groups of various kind; and consolidate the ancient practice of virgins consecrated in their own homes or the consecration of widows.[7]

The ascetic or monastic movement was similar to Montanism in its desire for a more austere life of penance and prayer, but there were differences. One was that the Montanists ordinarily did not separate themselves from the world to live a life of penance and prayerful solitude as the monks did, but more importantly, the mainstream of the monastic movement was unswervingly loyal to the Catholic church—her teaching and disciplines. The warm relationship between St. Athanasius, bishop of the illustrious see of Alexandria, and the Egyptian monastic movement demonstrates how Christians of different positions in the church possessing different charisms were intended by the Lord to respect and love each other. Satan's motto is certainly "divide and conquer"; the Holy Spirit always builds unity based on truth and virtue.

Later, as the ascetic movement spread and developed, other monks emerged as leaders of the movement. St. Basil of Caesarea authored a famous rule (actually both short and long rules) for the life of the monks, and in the West, St. Benedict of Nursia developed a moderate rule for monks that focused on a balanced life of prayer and work (*ora et labora*) in community, avoiding extremes and encouraging the use of a variety of charisms for the good of the church. The monasteries that followed St. Benedict's rule (Benedictine monasticism) became centers of Christian life and of the preservation and transmission of culture for decades and even centuries.

Though his "rule" changed history, St. Benedict was not a pretentious person. He simply wanted to give to the church a fervent, ascetic form of Christian life that many could follow in order to lead them to salvation. ("If you keep the Rule; the Rule will keep you.") Benedict responded to God's grace and call in his own life, and because of this faithful and obedient response, his order contributed greatly to the continued renewal of the church.

Renewal of Renewal

Another lesson that the church's history provides is that movements or groups that emerged to renew the church eventually are themselves in need of renewal in order to remain effective in witnessing to Christ and in building up the church. In order to understand this, let's seek to formulate some dynamics of renewal.

One of these would be simply that the Holy Spirit is always acting to renew the church or some aspect of the church's life. A movement becomes "institutionalized" as it becomes part of the church's normal life and as some structure emerges. Over the course of time a typical renewal movement either disappears or becomes integrated into the church's normal life. In the latter case the institutionalized movement can lose some of its initial fervor and thereby cease to be an effective force for the church's ongoing renewal. Many religious communities, founded to renew the church, continue to serve the church and preserve the heritage and charism of their origins, but they become less vibrant, and their mission less clear, over time. Thus what began as a renewal might need to be itself renewed in order to be a more effective source of grace for its members and of service to the church and to the world.

There were a number of periods or "waves" of monastic renewal in the Middle Ages. In the ninth and tenth centuries, there was a period of economic decline, political disintegration, and social instability in Europe: the so-called Dark Ages. At the beginning of the tenth century (around AD 910), a renewal of monastic life began at a monastery at Cluny, France. Through the leadership of the abbot, the monks returned to a more faithful observance of the rule of St. Benedict. The result was the formation of the first monastic order, in that for the first time monasteries placed themselves under the authority of another monastery and pledged themselves to observe the Benedictine rule in the same way as did Cluny.

"By 1100, three hundred monasteries were allied with Cluny; a century later, that number had multiplied five times to fifteen hundred monasteries." This steady growth can be credited largely to the charism and fidelity "of three abbots who oversaw Cluny and their affiliated monasteries for 155 years: Maieul (954–994), Odilo (994–1048), and Hugh (1049–1109)."[8]

Another author wrote: "Cluny exerted a considerable influence on the general renewal of the life of the Church, through the creation and multiplication throughout Europe of monastic communities of different sizes…which grew up around the Benedictine abbeys."[9]

But the renewal of monasticism did not end there. About two centuries after the founding of Cluny, an abbot, Robert of Molesme (1028–1112), felt that Clunaic monasticism, too, had grown lax and affluent, departing from the true practice of St. Benedict's rule. So in 1098 Robert led twenty other monks and founded a new monastery in an isolated spot called Cîteaux, south of Dijon in present-day France. Called Cistercians, these monks sought to renew monastic life by returning to its original simplicity in liturgy, focus on manual labor, and search for personal conversion through a life of prayer, solitude, and withdrawal from the world, as had the first desert fathers.

This cloistered, extremely ascetic Cistercian approach to monastic life was most widely spread by St. Bernard of Clairvaux, whose life exemplifies the power of personal charism. When he went to join the Cistercians around AD 1112, he influenced thirty young noblemen of Burgundy, including his own brothers, to enter the monastery with him. Bernard's leadership gifts were so evident that he was soon sent to found a new monastery and serve as its abbot, though he was young and inexperienced.[10] (It often happens that God uses the young and the weak to renew the church; see 1 Corinthians 1:26–29; 1 Timothy 4:12).

Paradoxically, the wisdom and gifts of this leader of the renewal of cloistered contemplative life led him to become both well-known and well-traveled. He reconciled warring political factions and preached the Second Crusade at the pope's behest. He was also embroiled in theological disputes, especially opposing the growing rationalism in theology represented by Peter Abelard. In engaging in these worldly activities and concerns, St. Bernard was obedient to the church and to the Lord, but his deepest desire was for prayer and contemplation. His writings represent the climax of the great monastic tradition that began in the fourth century, and for this he is called "the last of the [church] Fathers."

Regarding renewal, St. Bernard presented sound advice to his monks on the importance of receiving the inspiration and gifts of the Holy Spirit and of benefiting from these blessings oneself before going out to share them with others. In one of his most famous series of sermons, his *Commentary on the Song of Songs*, Bernard distinguishes between two operations of the Holy Spirit. The first he calls "infusion,…by which he [the Holy Spirit] inwardly strengthens the virtues that lead to [our own] salvation," such as "faith, hope and charity." The second he calls "effusion, by which [the Spirit] outwardly endows us with serviceable gifts," such as "the gift of wise and learned speech, the power to heal, [and] to prophesy," which are "used for our neighbor's salvation."

Bernard explains that we must not give to others what God has given to us for our good; nor must we keep for ourselves what

God has given us for the good of others. He also tells the monks to be "totally permeated by the infusion of the Holy Spirit" before "you rashly proceed to pour out your unfulfilled self upon others." Bernard goes on:

> The man who is wise, therefore, will see his life as more like a reservoir than a canal. The canal simultaneously pours out what it receives; the reservoir retains the water till it is filled, then discharges the overflow without loss to itself.... Today there are many in the Church who act like canals, the reservoirs are far too rare. So urgent is the charity of those through whom the streams of heavenly doctrine flow to us, that they want to pour it forth before they have been filled....
>
> ...[God] wishes that infusion should precede the effusion, an infusion to the fullest capacity.... You too must learn to await this fullness before pouring out your gifts, do not try to be more generous than God. The reservoir resembles the fountain that runs to form a stream or spreads to form a pool only when its own waters are brimming over.... First be filled, and then control the outpouring. The charity that is benign and prudent does not flow outwards until it abounds within.[11]

Through their deep union with Christ, the whole monastic movement was a reservoir of spiritual life and power that contributed to the life of the church and its renewal for many centuries.

Vatican II's Decree on the Apostolate of the Laity supports Bernard's directive:

> Christ, sent by the Father, is the source of the Church's whole apostolate. Clearly then, the fruitfulness of the apostolate of lay people depends on their living union with Christ; as the Lord said himself: 'Whoever dwells in me and I in him bears

much fruit, for separated from me you can do nothing' (Jn 15:5). (*Apostolicam Actuositatem*, 4)

The Poverty Movement

The twelfth century was a notable time of transition for Europe and for the church. Increased trade and the emergence of a middle class of merchants and entrepreneurs caused an economic boom that resulted in rising affluence, even in the church. However, with material prosperity came strife and warfare among cities and a growing spiritual hunger. Some anticlerical groups arose, influenced by a new emergence of Gnostic or Manichean theology, which saw the material world as corrupt and the worldly Catholic church as an abomination.

Many monasteries had shared in the prosperity of the age, but a new generation desired to return to the original monastic way of life, marked by simple prayer and austere penance. There was also a yearning for a new form of Christian life that would not be isolated from the growing cities.

St. Dominic

In this situation of economic, social, and religious ferment of the late twelfth century, God raised up a few individuals who would renew and literally reshape the church. One of these was Dominic Guzman. As a young priest, he went with his bishop on a mission to convert the Albigensians, one of the heretical Gnostic groups who were leading many people away from the Catholic church. Dominic realized that the affluence of the bishop's retinue only confirmed the Albigensians' criticisms of the worldliness of the church. In response Dominic formed a new religious community, the Order of Preachers, whose life of gospel poverty would complement and illustrate their preaching of the gospel of Christ.

Dominic also stressed the need for education of his preachers to refute error.

This new religious community contributed significantly to the renewal of the church by providing a new model of gospel life, different from monastic orders in that its mission was to preach and teach in the world. Because of the church's moratorium on new religious rules, Dominic adopted the Rule of St. Augustine for his order. This was well suited to it because Augustine had designed his rule for diocesan clergy, whose ministries were directed toward people in the world.

St. Francis of Assisi

In the history of the Catholic church there is probably no single person, next to Jesus, who caught the imagination of his age and revitalized the life of the church as much as Francis of Assisi. Francis was a layperson, son of a well-to-do cloth merchant, who as a young man was known as a spendthrift and the life of the party. God gradually revealed to Francis another way to live. He began to change during a long illness. Later he left Assisi to gain renown as a knight, but after having a heavenly vision, he turned back from battle and returned home.

Francis' father did not know what to make of his son. He became enraged when Francis gave away large sums of his money to the poor. Francis eventually sought the protection of the bishop and renounced all worldly possessions. The same words of Jesus about poverty and discipleship that caused St. Antony of Egypt to become a solitary ascetic moved St. Francis. Now, as a "knight for Christ," the chivalrous young man desired to devote himself entirely to the service of a new lady, Lady Poverty, and to imitate the poor Christ.

This personal call of God to Francis took a new turn one day when he was praying in the abandoned Church of San Damiano on the outskirts of Assisi. The figure of Christ on the crucifix spoke to him: "Francis, go and repair [*or* rebuild] my house, which, as you see, is falling completely into ruin." St. Bonaventure recounts how Francis "prepared to obey, gathering himself together to carry out the command of repairing the church materially, although the principal intention of the words referred to that Church which *Christ purchased with his own blood* (Acts 20:28), as the Holy Spirit taught him and as he himself later disclosed to the friars."[12]

Francis collected stones to rebuild San Damiano, often begging for them. The Lord overcame Francis' deep revulsion to lepers, which resulted in a unique ministry of personal care for these social outcasts.

Other men were attracted to Francis' simple way of life. When the number of his companions had grown to about a dozen, he decided that they should all journey to Rome to seek the approval of Pope Innocent III for the way of life they were leading. Francis' initial rule of 1209 was nothing more than a few texts of Jesus' teaching from the gospel. At first the pope was reluctant to approve such an austere rule, but Cardinal John of St. Paul replied, "If we reject this poor man's request on such a pretext, would not this be to declare that the Gospel cannot be practiced, and so to blaspheme Christ, its Author?"[13]

The pope heeded the cardinal's words and gave Francis initial approval to lead his followers on the path of gospel poverty. They could also preach the Good News of Christ if they received permission of the local bishop, though their charism (unlike Dominic's) was not preaching but primarily the witness of a poor, simple way of life in imitation of Jesus.

Initially the reception that Francis received from other religious and some citizens of Assisi was harsh. He accepted this persecution with such faith and good cheer that he began to win acceptance and even respect. He was totally unlike many of the other reformers of the time, who railed against the sins and worldliness of the church. He profoundly venerated the sacraments, especially the Eucharist, church buildings, the clergy, and the Catholic faith. St. Bonaventure wrote of him:

> When the friars asked him to teach them to pray, he said: "When you pray, say 'Our Father...' (Luke 11:2), and 'We adore you, O Christ, in all your churches in the whole world and we bless you because by your holy cross you have redeemed the world.'" He also taught them to praise God in all creatures and from all creatures, to honor priests with special reverence and to firmly believe and simply profess the true faith as held and taught by the Holy Roman Church.[14]

This text alludes to Francis' love for creatures and indeed for all of God's creation—a stark and striking contrast to the many neo-Gnostic groups of the time who saw the whole material order as corrupt and evil. Francis was known for his sermons to the birds, the taming of the wolf of Gubbio, and other acts that showed him to be a friend and "brother" to all creatures. This is exemplified in his "Canticle of the Creatures," in which he addresses the sun, moon, water, fire, and even death as his brothers and sisters, fellow creatures of the one, all-good Creator.

The impact of the *Poverello* ("little poor man") has been profound. His influence in renewing the Catholic church of the time lay in two things: first, his life of radical gospel poverty—pursued out of his personal love of the poor Christ, who humbled himself to become incarnate and to suffer all the pains of humanity in his passion and death; and second, his absolute devotion to the Catholic church and everything Catholic. Everyone could see that Francis loved Jesus, lived like Jesus, and loved the church. His simple zeal was infectious and winning.

The secret of St. Francis' power to renew the church was his relationship with God, his prayer. Although his was an active life in the world, Francis (like Jesus) frequently withdrew from this for contemplation and prayer. St. Bonaventure observed:

> He was accustomed not to pass over negligently any visitation of the Spirit. When it was granted, he followed it and as long as the Lord allowed, he enjoyed the sweetness offered him. When he was on a journey and felt the breathing of the divine Spirit, letting his companions go on ahead, he would stand still and render this new inspiration fruitful, not *receiving the grace in vain* (2 Cor. 6:1). Many times he was lifted up in ecstatic contemplation so that, rapt out of himself and experiencing what is beyond human understanding, he was unaware of what went on about him....
>
> He had learned in prayer that the presence of the Holy Spirit for which he longed was granted more intimately to those who invoke him, the more the Holy Spirit found them withdrawn from the noise of worldly affairs. Therefore seeking out lonely places, he used to go to deserted areas and abandoned churches to pray at night.[15]

St. Bonaventure goes on to describe how in these prayer vigils Francis would be attacked, even physically, by devils, but these attacks made him even more courageous in prayer and in practicing virtue. The account is very similar to St. Athanasius' description of St. Antony of Egypt's battles with demons. Francis, in prayer, would weep, moan, shed tears "imploring the divine mercy for sinners and weeping for the Lord's passion."[16] Many frescoes of Francis portray him kneeling with arms outstretched, culminating in his receiving the wounds of Christ, the stigmata, while praying on Mount LaVerna toward the end of his life.

If there was any shortcoming in St. Francis, it was his impatience with and grief over those who wanted to mitigate the absolute poverty that he observed and which he desired his followers to practice. He wanted to live, and his followers to live, as Jesus taught, having "nowhere to lay his head" (Matthew 8:20), trusting in the Father's provision as do the birds and the lilies (Matthew 6:26–32). This was not practical, but Francis was not a bit concerned with this. He did not wish his order to own anything but simply to use whatever was given them.

After Francis' death there was division within the order. Some wanted to observe the strict poverty of Francis, as expressed in his final Testament, and others accepted the church's eventual judgment allowing the Franciscans to own property (and thus take responsibility for it) instead of just using what belonged to the church or members of the church.

As with all the saints, Francis was honored and imitated for living the gospel without compromise. This vision inspired many, allowed God's grace to be poured out, and renewed the church.

GOD'S INTERVENTIONS
Author Fidel González Fernández summarized the impact of the mendicant movement:

> The new mendicant orders were like a breath of fresh air reviving the Church. Numerous groups of men, full of illusion and

holy ambitions, wished to combat for Christ. The charisms of Dominic and Francis and of the other mendicants were a providential response to [the] needs [of the time], [a] unique, unexpected and mysterious gift of God to his Church. These great Saints involved themselves in the midst of...social crisis.... They were not responses excogitated in the study, but *miracles*, interventions of God in the history of man. Their life immediately appealed to people, who regarded them with astonishment and wished to follow them. Those who became their spiritual sons, and shared their charism, very soon became numerous. And from now on they would be the main protagonists of ecclesial life both in the history of theology and in the history of mission, virtually down to the sixteenth century, when God enriched the Church with other new and providential charisms that aroused new groups of faithful and inspired incisive movements of new ecclesial life.[17]

Fernández also points out that the "new" mendicant movement "did not wipe out the charisms of the monks or canons," because a "charism in the Church never cancels another charism; it always helps it to recover, to renew itself, to rediscover its genuine original identity."[18] This is generally true, though there are times when a religious order or a movement in the church has fulfilled its purpose in God's plan and may die out or become integrated into the life of the church. But more on this later.

St. Catherine of Siena and the Late Middle Ages

It is understandable, in studying the history of renewal in the church, for one to leap ahead from the mendicant renewal of the thirteenth century to the Catholic Reformation of the sixteenth century. The fourteenth and fifteenth centuries (until the

Renaissance) are generally regarded as a time of decline and struggle for the church, marked by the Avignon papacy and the Great Schism. But it is in such difficult times that renewal is most needed and desired. Whenever the church experiences difficulty, the faithfulness of God is revealed in those who respond to his grace and become agents of renewal.

Catherine of Siena stands out as one of these beacons of light in a difficult age. In the fourteenth century the papacy had moved to Avignon, France, where it was criticized for the affluence of its court and suspected of being beholden to French interests. Catherine of Siena would be considered one of the least likely people to influence the pope to return to Rome and to renew the church, but that is exactly what she did.

Catherine's zeal for God began when she was a young child. Her "excessive" piety led her parents to heap chores on her and to ridicule her devotion. Catherine accepted this and grew more fervent in prayer, joining the Third Order Dominicans at age sixteen. Her parents finally relented and gave her a private room in their home, where she prayed and fasted, leaving the house only to attend Mass.

When Catherine was twenty-one, God unexpectedly called her out of her home to work among the sick, to whom she devoted herself tirelessly. Her reputation for holiness, wisdom, and asceticism grew, and many followed her example, forming a joyful community under her direction. *The Dialogue* is Catherine's most famous spiritual writing, and it merited her recognition as a doctor of the church in 1970 by Pope Paul VI, along with St. Teresa of Avila.

For the last five years of her life, Catherine was called to a more public ministry in the church, settling disputes and urging

Pope Gregory XI to return the papal court to Rome, which he finally did in 1378. However, shortly thereafter he died, and a dispute arose concerning the succession of the papacy—the Great Schism. Catherine returned to Rome, seeking the reunification of the church, but died there at age thirty-three, grief-stricken over the situation.[19] Though her life ended in apparent failure in the cause of church unity, her zeal for spiritual growth, her care for the sick, and her concern for the unity of the church form a particularly shining witness of renewal in a dark time in the church's life.

The fourteenth century was also when the Black Death swept through Europe, killing between a quarter and a half of the population in some regions. This, along with the Avignon papacy and the Great Schism, led to a weakening of the pastoral ministry of the Catholic church, which caused people to seek remedies for the church and themselves that were often extreme. Some, like John Wycliffe in England and Jan Hus in Prague, broke away from the church and took followers (the Lollards and the Hussites) with them. Others became millenarians, predicting that the end of the world was imminent.

Many others sought to encounter God within their hearts, instructed by the writings and teachings of mystics. Each region of Europe produced significant Catholic mystics in this period. They contributed to a necessary spiritual strengthening and renewal, though their writings varied in real spiritual wisdom and were closely monitored by church leaders.

One fascinating renewal movement in this period (which was less mystical and more practical than most) was a group known as the Brethren of the Common Life, founded in the Netherlands by Gerhard Groote in the late fourteenth century. "He demanded no vows from his disciples, but left them free, whether clerics or laymen, to continue in their ordinary vocations. His followers developed a lofty spirituality."[20]

This spirituality is reflected in the movement's most famous work, *The Imitation of Christ*, by Thomas à Kempis. The pursuit of holiness in everyday life, focusing on charity, prayer, and practical imitation of the life of Jesus Christ, is the hallmark of this spirituality, which was known at the time as the *devotio moderna* ("modern devotion"). In an age of spiritual confusion and social turmoil, this spirituality, lived with communal support, certainly was a leaven in the church. Its members were especially known for their schools and educational work, offered without charge.

The Brethren's most famous center was started by Groote at Deventer, but their schools spread throughout the Netherlands and into Germany. Pope Hadrian VI had been involved with the Brethren, and Nicholas of Cusa, Rudolph Agricola, and later Erasmus (of Rotterdam) attended their schools. From the small gathering of Groote's followers, this community grew to be another powerful source of strength and renewal for the church in the late Middle Ages.[21]

The Catholic Reformation of the Sixteenth and Seventeenth Centuries
From the church's first centuries there has not been such a plethora and variety of Catholic saints and new spiritualities as are found in the sixteenth and seventeenth centuries. The church in this period was embroiled in its greatest crisis since the eleventh-century East-West schism: the Protestant Reformation.

Despite the few hopeful signs of renewal in the late Middle Ages, the Catholic church entered the sixteenth century in dire need for reform from laxity, worldliness, corruption, and other ills. Some church leaders recognized this, as we will discuss in the next chapter. Among those in the church who spoke out boldly against the abuses was the Dominican priest Girolamo Savonarola of Florence. As prior of his community, he prophetically denounced certain practices of the Roman Curia and of Pope Alexander VI. Though many Florentines revered Savonarola as a holy man and a true reformer, he was excommunicated in 1497 and hanged a year later in the market square of Florence as a schismatic and a heretic.[22]

The failure of the church to reform herself in time or sufficiently was one cause of the Protestant Reformation. This tragic schism is interpreted by some as God's judgment on the Catholic church, and yet the tremendous number of people whom God raised up to renew the church in this period demonstrates God's great fidelity to the church and illustrates the principle that where sin abounds, grace abounds all the more (see Romans 5:20).

It would be difficult to mention here all of the movements of God's grace that renewed the Catholic church in this period; that would be a book in itself. To illustrate what God was doing, let us consider the lives of three saints of the Catholic Reformation—St. Ignatius of Loyola, St. Teresa of Avila, and St. Philip Neri—and the power of the personal charism that each of them possessed.

St. Ignatius of Loyola

Ignatius of Loyola exemplified renewal in this period in that he was a layman who experienced a powerful religious conversion that led to his developing a whole new form of Catholic life and a new type of religious community. Ignatius' life shows, once again, the originality and uniqueness of the Holy Spirit's action; there is nothing scripted about his call from God. Here is a vain, noble soldier whose leg is badly broken by a cannonball, yet he insists on having it broken again and reset because he wants it to look better. In his convalescence all that is available to read is a life of Jesus and a biography of some saints. After having a vision of the Madonna with her Child, he begins to think about redirecting his life: "Suppose I did what St. Francis or St. Dominic did?"[23]

While meditating on the difference in the "feelings" he has after daydreaming about doing feats of arms and then about serving Christ as the saints did, Ignatius stumbles upon the key principles of his famous method of discernment of spirits. This concept is developed in a year spent in severe penance at Manresa. He travels to Rome to meet the pope, then journeys as a pilgrim to the Holy Land. As no clear idea of his vocation develops, he decides, at age thirty-three, that he must study in order to be useful to souls.

So the zealous Basque goes to school in Barcelona, Alcala, and finally in Salamanca, where he is scrutinized by the Inquisition. Though acquitted, Ignatius realizes that he is not achieving his goal in Spain. He knows little French, yet he decides to study in Paris. There he comes

> to realize that the spiritual knowledge he had acquired at Manresa must be associated with other forms of learning, such as are obtained by study and hard work. At Alcala and Salamanca he had been in too much of a hurry.... Despite his maturity he had the wisdom and strength of mind to spend no fewer than seven years rebuilding his [intellectual] foundations.

This extended intellectual preparation is so valued by Ignatius that it later becomes a mandatory part of the formation of his followers.[24]

So here is the ex-soldier, at age forty a penurious student twice the age of many of his peers, who often is compelled to beg in order to continue his education. This aging, limping scholar comes to be respected and then consulted by a few students. Some of them are allowed to study Ignatius' *Spiritual Exercises*. One reluctant convert is an athletic, ambitious young nobleman named Francis Xavier, who initially thinks Ignatius is just an unusual character but eventually is won over by his frequently posed question: "What does it profit a man, to gain the whole world and forfeit his life?" (Mark 8:36).[25]

The result of Ignatius of Loyola's years of labor was the formation of a band of seven men, the Company of Jesus, who made vows of perpetual poverty, chastity, obedience, and loyalty to the pope. They did this on the "Hill of Martyrs," *Montmartre*, just outside Paris, on August 15, 1534. Six years later in Rome, Pope Paul III canonically established the Society of Jesus as an order with strict military discipline pledged to be totally at the disposal of the pope. It was different from any previous active religious order in that there was no obligation to pray the Divine Office in common. Flexibility—the ability to adapt to any mission or apostolate—was the priority of the Jesuits.

By the time Ignatius died in 1556, the order had more than a thousand members serving the church as missionaries, educators, pastors, and apologists. The sons of St. Ignatius were the vanguard of the renewal of the church, the Catholic Reformation.[26] "One can say—without fear of contradiction…that it became the most powerful instrument of Catholic revival and resurgence in this era of religious crisis. Yet the dynamic element in the Order was and remained the experience of a Spanish saint," Ignatius of Loyola.[27]

What lessons in church renewal can we learn from St. Ignatius of Loyola and the early Jesuits?

First, Ignatius of Loyola was not a typical charismatic figure who immediately attracted attention and followers. There were thirteen years of labor, prayer, study, and self-denial between his conversion and the emergence of the little band of seven at Montmartre. There were six more years before the rule of the society was approved.[28] St. Ignatius of Loyola teaches us that receiving a personal charism or a special grace or call is not enough to renew the church. He had to persevere through trial and faithfully follow God's call, one step at a time, before seeing tangible results. Often a renewal led by an individual takes time to have an impact. The formula "charism + labor = renewal" applies here.

Further,

> the Society of Jesus in turn generated other movements: it gave rise to the Marian congregations, to the Movement of Friendship in France and not less than a thousand religious institutes and institutes of consecrated life of every kind, that were either founded by Jesuits or inspired by the experience of grace and by the spirituality of Ignatius of Loyola.[29]

St. Teresa of Avila

While Ignatius ignited renewal through founding a new religious order, another Spaniard, Teresa of Avila (or Teresa of Jesus), brought renewal through the reform of an established order, the Carmelites. Both Ignatius and Teresa were spiritual masters whose contributions to understanding and living the Christian faith were as important as their work with their respective religious communities.

Teresa's life is an inspiring lesson in the persistence of God's mercy and renewing grace. An intelligent, attractive girl, she was inclined from her youth to enter religious life and was educated for a time in a convent school. Against her father's wishes she entered the local Carmelite Convent of the Incarnation at age twenty. The convent was not very strict, and the nuns were able to travel and receive visitors. It was a comfortable life. A mysterious illness caused Teresa to return home to recuperate, but after three years she reentered and led a rather relaxed religious life until she was almost forty years old.

Then a profound change occurred in Teresa. Some say it was looking at a statue of Jesus' scourging that awakened in her an awareness of God's love for her and of her lukewarmness toward God. She began to pray single-heartedly and was blessed with mystical graces, including visions and interior locutions from God.

Through good spiritual direction and her own innate common sense, Teresa was able to discern different stages of growth in union with God. These she explained in her autobiography (written under obedience) and later in a number of books that have become spiritual classics, including *The Way of Perfection* and *Interior Castle*, in which she describes seven "mansions" one inhabits at different stages of spiritual growth. "As a spiritual writer her influence was epoch-making, because she was the first to point to...states of prayer intermediate between discursive meditation and ecstasy ('quiet' and 'union') and...the entire life of prayer from meditation to the so-called mystic marriage" to Christ, which she experienced in 1572.[30] For this she was declared a doctor of the church by Pope Paul VI in 1970.

St. Teresa's contribution to the renewal of the church is also seen in her desire to reform the spiritual life of the Carmelite order. In 1562, in the face of strong opposition, she established the Convent of St. Joseph in Avila. Those who joined her and those who followed her reform elsewhere were known as Discalced (barefoot) Carmelites because of their strict poverty and discipline.

In 1567 Teresa met a short, young Carmelite named John, who was about to join the Carthusians (the strictest monastic order) because he was disillusioned with the lack of fervor in the Carmelites. Teresa convinced him to join her in seeking to renew the Carmelite order, which he did. John also was a mystic and a poet, and his focus was on the encounter with God in "darkness," in times of abandonment and suffering. His religious name, John of the Cross, bespeaks this, as do the suffering and persecution that he, along with Teresa, endured in pursuing the Carmelite reform. In 1575 the Carmelite order called a halt to the Discalced reforms in Spain, leading to John's imprisonment in a dark, narrow cell, where he lived on bread and water for nine months. There he wrote most of his *Spiritual Canticle*, one of the greatest poems in Spanish and Christian literature.

In 1580 Pope Gregory XIII lifted the ban on the Discalced Carmelites and allowed them to govern themselves. The renewal of the order was recognized and affirmed by the church's highest authority. It is fitting yet tragic that St. John of the Cross died in 1591 in great suffering, after being banished to Andalusia by the vicar general of the Carmelites for insisting on further reforms.

St. Teresa labored for the last twenty years of her life leading the Discalced Carmelite renewal. In spite of many trials, she was known for her joy and equanimity. Like St. Francis of Assisi and St. Philip Neri, she believed that "long-faced saints...make both virtue and themselves abhorrent."[31] By the time of her death at age sixty-seven in 1582, she and John had founded seventeen reformed convents with over two hundred sisters and ten discalced men's monasteries with approximately three hundred friars.[32]

Both their mystical writings and their renewal of religious life have made a lasting impact on the church. It is notable that this renewal all began with Teresa of Avila, when at age forty she entered into a deeper prayer life—a deeper relationship with the Lord. Her charism of mystical prayer overflowed into her writings and into her active life as a foundress of a new branch of the Carmelites. Once again the renewal of the church was sparked by one who sought God and his kingdom first.

It should be noted that other religious communities were renewed during the Catholic Reformation. Among the largest and most influential of these was the Capuchin order (O.F.M. CAP.), a Franciscan community started by Matteo (Matthew) di Bassi (or da Bascio) of Urbino, Italy, in 1529. Like the Discalced Carmelites, the Capuchins were opposed by other Franciscans and were almost suppressed when their third general, Bernard Ochino, left the Catholic church. "But their enthusiastic preaching and missionary work gained them popular support,"[33] as did their embrace of greater poverty, lived out (in their early years) in little communities of simple huts in the countryside or mountains. After 1572 they were allowed to found houses outside of Italy, and eventually they were second only to the Jesuits in their influence as a religious order in the Catholic Reformation period.[34]

St. Philip Neri

In listing the great renewal figures of the Catholic Reformation, St. Philip Neri is easy to overlook. He did not leave behind a body of profound spiritual writings nor start a powerful, unified religious order. The charism of Philip Neri was a deep and vibrant holiness that powerfully affected those around him, so much so that he has been called the "Second Apostle of Rome."

How Philip arrived in Rome and developed a following and an apostolate there is a fascinating tale. He was born in Florence, but at age eighteen he was sent away to learn business from his father's cousin. Instead of finding his vocation as a businessman, Philip developed a deep prayer life under the direction of a holy monk of the Benedictine abbey of Monte Cassino and through reading, especially the life of Blessed Colombini (who always spoke of Jesus) and the *Laudi* ("Praises") of Jacopone da Todi. After a few months he bade his "uncle" farewell and went to Rome dressed as a poor pilgrim.

In Rome Philip lodged with a customs agent and tutored the man's two sons. He took a few courses in philosophy and theology but spent most of his time in prayer. He soon abandoned his studies all together and lived as a hermit in the middle of the city. He made regular pilgrimages to the seven churches of Rome and to the catacombs, meditating on Christ and his passion and living on a meager diet. He loved solitude.

Then, on Pentecost 1544, Philip's life changed radically. His first biographer, Gallonio, recorded:

> It was habitual with Philip to pray each day to the Holy Spirit, and with great humility to ask Him for His gifts and graces.... [That day, while he was praying in the Catacomb of St. Sebastian,] he suddenly felt himself divinely filled with the power of the Spirit with such force that his heart began to palpitate within his body and to be inflamed with such love that ...he indicated that he was completely unable to bear it.[35]

Philip never spoke much of his own experiences of God, but in his last years he told a close friend that he had seen, at his Pentecost event, a ball of fire enter his mouth and had felt it go down into his breast. After his death an autopsy revealed an expanded heart with the adjacent ribs broken outward. However, the truly important result was that, as Cardinal Frederick Borromeo testified, Philip's prayer to be an instrument of the Holy Spirit and to receive his gifts had been answered in a remarkable way.[36]

Philip's "Pentecost" marked the beginning of a unique apostolate that contributed to the renewal of the church in Rome and affected the universal church as well. As time went on Philip became more involved with "fraternities"—groups primarily composed of laypeople like himself who devoted themselves to spiritual growth and prayer and to works of mercy, especially care of the sick. These groups originated with the teaching of Caterina Adorno—St. Catherine of Genoa—and the work of prominent Genoese layman Ettore Vernazza, who in 1497 started the Oratory of Divine Love in Genoa. Between 1514 and 1517 a branch of this Oratory was founded in Rome and signaled "the beginning of effective Catholic reform in this troubled age."[37] Two members of the Roman Oratory were Bishop Gian Carafa (later Pope Paul IV) and St. Gaetano da Thiene, who founded the Theatine order of priests in 1524.[38]

Because of the power of Philip's personal charism, he went from being a member of these fraternities to being considered the founder of the Oratory that later bore his name. As noted Catholic historian Henri Daniel-Rops has written:

> In the little church of S. Girolamo della Carità, or rather in the
> crypt of that church, he used to receive his friends, who met

together as fervent souls in quest of truth and virtue. This little group was known as the Oratory, one of the most singular institutions (at least in its beginnings) ever recognized by the Catholic Church. With characteristic spontaneity Philip gave rise to a new method of spiritual exercises entirely different from that of St. Ignatius. A free verbal commentary, it was called *Oratorio*, and gave its name to one of the most beautiful forms of religious music. One of the brethren began by reading a passage from some edifying book. Another explained and commented upon this text. A third asked questions, put forward objections and elucidated such points as were still obscure. But one must never remain too long upon the dizzy heights of speculation; so another member would narrate an episode of ecclesiastical history, while another recalled day by day the events of Our Lord's life. Philip presided; at every stage he would interject some remark or observation, and it was always he who rounded off the discussion. After this the meeting broke up, hurried down the steps of the church and started in procession through the streets. Then they all went to pray in the catacombs, or perhaps from St. Peter's to St. John Lateran, from San Lorenzo to the basilica of Santa Croce, which preserves the memory of the crusaders. As they walked they sang with alternate voice those splendid antiphons which had lately been set to glorious music by a brilliant composer named Palestrina.

It is quite certain that Philip had at this time no idea whatever of founding an Order. He would have been astonished to learn that he was in fact doing so. . . .

. . . [I]n spite of Philip's hesitation and resistance, the Oratory came into being, and groups were established at such places as Naples, Milan, Lucca, Fermo and Bologna. At Naples the institution was well organized, at Lucca and Fermo hardly at all; in no case was there more than the slenderest link with that of Rome. Nor was it until 1575, by express order of the Pope, that Philip allowed his free movement to become a congregation. The new congregation, however, was unique: clerics and pious laymen were to pray and work in common, subject to a very simple rule which imposed no external discipline or strict regulations. It was to be a republic controlled by Love, wholly different from the Society of Jesus. The one and only tie acknowledged and proclaimed was "that born of mutual affection and daily intercourse"; and when Philip was asked what was the sum total of his Rule, he answered quite simply, grave yet smiling: "Nothing but charity."

Nevertheless this first Oratory, whimsical and unorganized though it was, exerted considerable influence and produced many men who distinguished themselves in the great struggles of that age.[39]

So St. Philip Neri, with his humor and spontaneity, attracted people in Rome of every rank and class to Jesus Christ and his gospel and thus served to promote the renewal of the church in a time of great crisis. One of the most famous members of the Oratory in another time of crisis, the nineteenth century, was John Henry Newman, the Anglican convert to Catholicism who, after becoming a Catholic priest, established an Oratory at Old Oscott (Birmingham, England) in 1848.

Joy was a defining characteristic of St. Philip Neri. His cheerful exhortations: *"Allegrammente!* Be cheerful!" and "Well, brothers, when shall we begin to do good?" motivated people to follow him and to imitate his life of prayer and service.[40] As a modern biographer wrote: "Joy is one of the special gifts of the Holy Spirit. In the Process of Canonization we are continually coming across testimonies to the brightness, even the exuberance of joy, that flowed from the presence of the Spirit of God in Philip. Even in sickness he did not lose his inner serenity."[41]

From his first days in Rome, Philip regularly visited the sick in hospitals, and later he sent his companions and penitents to do the same. He met Ignatius of Loyola and St. Camillus de Lellis at the hospital of San Giacomo.[42]

Beyond the Seventeenth Century

In summary, during the sixteenth century the Holy Spirit poured out a remarkable variety of charisms for the renewal of the church in a difficult period. Apparently the many forms of renewal had an impact on the laity, at least in Catholic Spain, where half the books published between 1500 and 1670 concerned religion and where, in the early seventeenth century, over 80 percent of the population were able to recite by heart the Creed, the Ten Commandments, and basic prayers.[43]

Due to a so-called "Enlightenment," culminating in the French Revolution, the eighteenth century was a very difficult period for European Christianity and Christian missions. Nonetheless, the evangelical revival was a powerful movement of renewal within the Protestant world. It began in England and in Germany (there known as Pietism) and quickly spread to the British colonies in the New World.

The Catholic church did not experience a comparable blossoming of renewed ecclesial and spiritual life until the nineteenth century. This Catholic renewal took many forms, notably the founding of many religious orders (in which women often took a leading role) and Catholic missionary institutes and orders.[44] Some of the common themes in Catholic devotion were the pierced heart of Christ crucified, the exaltation of Christ the King, Mary the Immaculate Conception, and "constant reference …to the action of the Holy Spirit."[45]

However, this chapter is not a complete history of renewal. Let us look at the personal charism of two figures of the nineteenth century, one European and one American, who illustrate how God worked through individuals to renew the church. Both of these happen to be priests—Clarence Walworth, a Redemptorist, and St. John Bosco.

CLARENCE WALWORTH

Walworth is a representative of the itinerant clergy who sparked a nineteenth-century revival among Catholics in America through the parish mission. While the preaching of the typical Sunday homily was aimed at doctrinal instruction, the preaching of the parish mission was aimed at conversion. Jay P. Dolan's *Catholic Revivalism: The American Experience 1830–1900* is a fascinating study of the parish mission as a powerful source and instrument of renewal of the Catholic church in America in the nineteenth century. "The whole tenor of the mission," Dolan writes, "its ritual, its music, as well as its dramatic oratory…was geared to the goal of the conversion of sinners."[46]

Of course, this was also the goal of the Protestant evangelists, whom we tend to associate with "revival" preaching. But the Paulists, Jesuits, Redemptorists, and other orders who conducted parish missions had preachers of equal effectiveness. Dolan writes:

When Charles G. Finney, one of the premier Protestant revivalists of the nineteenth century, was writing his memoirs, he included [this] passage about a convert at his 1842 revival in Rochester [New York]:

Several of the lawyers that were at this time converted in Rochester, gave up their profession and went into the ministry. Among these was one of the Chancellor W——'s sons, at that time a young lawyer in Rochester, and who appeared at the time to be soundly converted. For some reason, with which I am not acquainted, he went to Europe and to Rome, and finally became a Roman Catholic priest. He has been for years laboring zealously to promote revivals of religion among them, holding protracted meetings; and, as he told me himself, when I met him in England, trying to accomplish in the Roman Catholic church what I was endeavoring to accomplish in the Protestant church…. When I was in England, he was there, and sought me out, and came very affectionately to see me; and we had just as pleasant an interview, so far as I know, as we should have had, if we had both been Protestants. He said nothing of his peculiar views, but only that he was laboring among the Roman Catholics to promote revivals of religion.

The person to whom Finney referred was Clarence Walworth, lawyer, convert, Roman Catholic priest and one of the foremost parish mission preachers in nineteenth-century Catholic America.

…The religion of revivalism was not exclusively a Protestant enterprise, but it also swept through Catholic America in the second half of the nineteenth century and, in the process, shaped the piety of the people and strengthened the institutional church.[47]

As Walworth himself said, "There is no time like the time of the mission...to attend to the 'great affair' of salvation. Pray now for it is a time of mercy, the time of the mission; pray now, tonight, for tomorrow it may be too late to pray."[48]

The charism of preaching, which was so central to the parish mission, made a great impact on the life of the Catholic church in America. Dolan summarizes:

> In the 1840s the itinerant preacher was a rare species and the Catholic revival meeting an uncommon event. By the end of the century organized groups of preachers crisscrossed the nation preaching a brand of religion that had become an integral ingredient of Catholic piety. The parish mission was a common occurrence which the hierarchy promoted, religious orders popularized and people supported. The revival meeting had become an accepted feature of parish life, a standard event scheduled to occur at regular intervals to boom up the religion of the people.[49]

The impact of a parish mission on the local church and community is exemplified by the public ceremony that closed many parish missions in the nineteenth century: the erection of the mission cross in a prominent place. The account of this ceremony in Loretto, Pennsylvania, recounted by Isaac Hecker (founder of the Paulist Fathers) in a letter to Orestes Brownson on May 15, 1851, is quite moving:

> I must describe to you in a few words the closing ceremony, the plantation of the cross. We all assembled in the church on Sunday afternoon at 3:30 to recite the Rosary. The procession then was formed outside the Church. First came the proces-

sional cross with the boys, then the men carrying a large cross 40 feet long entwined with garlands of flowers borne by 60 of them; on each side of the cross was a file of soldiers with a band of music; then came 20 or 30 Franciscan brothers of the third order with their cowls; then the clergy; after them the missioners in their habit, followed by the Sisters of Mercy, and these by the girls and women. The number of the procession was about 4,000. We marched through the village to the site of the cross with music, and there we blessed and erected the cross in a most conspicuous place. The farewell sermon was preached at the foot of the cross and the papal Benediction given. It was a novel scene for America, a famous one for our holy religion, and one which never will be forgotten by those who witnessed it. The cross overlooks the whole village, and when you look that way you will always see some one or more saying their five paters and aves to gain the indulgence of 10,000 years which is attached to the missionary cross.[50]

ST. JOHN BOSCO

Another example of the power of personal charism in the renewal of the church is the work of St. John Bosco in nineteenth-century Italy. Don Bosco's evident charism was the ability to attract and work with youth, especially catechizing them—instructing them in the truths of the Catholic faith. One biographer wrote: "His hold upon the hearts of the young was almost irresistible. One day he…successfully achieved the astounding feat of making a whole day's excursion with three hundred juvenile offenders, whom he took out of Turin, without any assistance from the police, and then brought quietly back to their cells."[51]

John Bosco spent twenty months trying to find a place to meet with the hundreds of youths who followed him. This was in addition to helping them find work, hearing their confessions, entertaining them, and keeping them fed and clothed. He was forced to move five times in ten months. Finally he caught pneumonia and nearly died. After his recovery he gradually gained support, and three oratories for youth were founded in Turin.

At Christmastime in 1849 John Bosco began a parish mission that was intended for all the boys in Turin. This weeklong event was so successful, as measured by confessions and general interest, that it was continued for many years. The missions were given by preachers whom Don Bosco knew could reach the boys.

In 1854 cholera broke out in the city, killing hundreds. The city lacked enough medical personnel to care for the sick, much less seek them out, as many were abandoned and alone. St. John Bosco enlisted the help of forty young men. "For more than two months those forty young fellows were absolutely run off their legs. And yet not one of them was attacked by the disease. The protection of the Blessed Virgin Mary was visibly over them."[52]

St. John Bosco's dedication and zeal for youth is a remarkable model for church renewal. The congregation he founded, the Salesians of Don Bosco, and the "preventive system" of working joyfully with youth according to the principles of reason, religion, and (loving) kindness, continue his work and spirit to the present day. His motto, "Give me souls—the rest matters nothing," reveals the single-heartedness of his dedication, based on unshakable faith in Jesus Christ and the help of the Blessed Virgin Mary.

It is often said that the youth are the future of the church. If this is so, St. John Bosco's life and principles provide valuable lessons for securing that future for God's glory.

Conclusion

What can we learn from this "sample" of the variety of personal charisms, the gifts of the Holy Spirit, that God has bestowed on his church through the ages? Each individual mentioned provides many lessons. What is evident, in general, is that God wills and provides for the ongoing renewal of his people through the abundance of gifts that Christians receive (see 1 Corinthians 12:7). The renewal of the church depends on the recognition, the wholehearted acceptance, and the committed use of these gifts, guided by pastors and others whose gift is to discern and guide the different gifts. Those who have been most effective in promoting the church's renewal—many of whom have been declared saints through the canonization process—are those whose lives have been dedicated to using their charisms for the service of the church and others.

Another lesson is that those who dedicate themselves to the renewal of the church often experience setbacks, difficulties, misunderstanding, and even persecution. We also see that renewal often occurs after many years of persevering, patient toil by those who are following God's call. In the furnace of affliction, the "gold" of renewal is purified, and the weak or impure is destroyed.

Finally, it is striking to see just how creative God is in raising up new leaders, with unique calls and charisms, to renew the church. As G.K. Chesterton put it, it is heresies that are dull and unexciting, but the "wild truth" thunders through the corridors of history, "reeling but erect."[53]

This is a challenge, certainly, for those responsible for discerning and ordering charisms—those whose gift and call is to oversee the church and its renewal. It is this office that will be discussed in the next chapter.

CHAPTER FIVE

The Influence of Ecclesial Office

God's grace at work in particular individuals is not enough to bring about renewal, even if the individuals are responding whole-heartedly to that grace and seeking to carry out the mission the Lord has entrusted to them. In order for a grace or charism to renew the church, it must be recognized, accepted, and approved by the proper ecclesiastical authorities, the church's pastors. (In the Catholic church the primary pastors are the bishops, including the church's chief and universal pastor or shepherd, the pope.)

Otherwise bearers of charisms can divide or weaken the church, as in the case of Montanus, Peter Waldo (or Valdes), Martin Luther, and many others. We do not deny that these individuals may have had genuine calls and gifts to renew the church. But when they encountered questions and correction from ecclesiastical authorities, they refused to respond and submit. They left the Catholic church and founded new groups.

Here our focus is not on those who left the Catholic church but on the Catholic ecclesial authorities responsible for this church's guidance, particularly the bishops and the pope.

Principles to Be Observed
Church leaders have two responsibilities when it comes to discerning renewal efforts: to preserve the unity of the church and to promote its authentic renewal. Based on the belief that Jesus Christ founded only one church on earth, which is clearly the teaching of the New Testament (see Matthew 16:18; John 10:16; 17:20–23, and elsewhere), the church's leaders must ensure that all efforts of reform or renewal also protect and promote the unity of the church.

The Pauline writings emphasize this. The Christians in Ephesus are exhorted to forbear one another in love, "eager to maintain the unity of the Spirit in the bond of peace."

> There is one body and one Spirit, just as you were called to the one hope that belongs to your call, one Lord, one faith, one baptism, one God and Father of us all, who is above all and through all and in all. But grace was given to each of us according to the measure of Christ's gift....
>
> And his gifts were that some should be apostles, some prophets, some evangelists, some pastors and teachers, to equip the saints for the work of ministry, for building up the body of Christ, until we all attain to the unity of the faith and of the knowledge of the Son of God.... Speaking the truth in love, we are to grow up in every way into him who is the head, into Christ, from whom the whole body, joined and knit together by every joint with which it is supplied, when each part is working properly, makes the body grow and upbuilds itself in love. (Ephesians 4:3–7, 11–13, 15–16)

The Pauline theology teaches that the church is one body composed of members who all have particular and diverse charisms (gifts) that are to be used to promote the growth and unity of the body of Christ. This continues until the church finally attains its full stature: when it grows into the fullness of Christ in the glory of heaven. In the meantime one of the chief responsibilities of the church's leaders is to guide her in this path of unity, seeing that all the gifts and graces given to the members of the church are used in a way that fosters that unity, not threatens or undermines it.

However, if preserving unity were the only concern of the church's leaders, the task could be relatively easy. Anything that appeared to "rock the boat" or threaten the existing unity (the status quo) could be suppressed. This is not St. Paul's vision. The church is a body alive with a multitude of charisms, which the Holy Spirit pours out so that the body will grow into the fullness of Christ, the Head. This growth continues until the end of human history, when the church is perfected and her marriage to Christ is celebrated in the glory of heaven (see Revelation 21).

We don't want a human body to stop growing: Throughout life a person grows (or should grow) physically, emotionally, intellectually, morally, and spiritually. Even when other growth ceases, a person still grows in wisdom, which comes through reflection with age and experience. The church too is a living, growing body that is constantly being renewed. Hence the church will experience "growing pains."

So the second responsibility of church leaders is to promote, actively, the church's renewal. This is done by the leaders either personally undertaking action to renew her or encouraging those members of the church (or even, at times, those outside the church) who are striving to use their gifts and vision for the church's renewal. This encouragement might include constructive guidance of the members' efforts for renewal.

The key is not to stifle the Holy Spirit, even as he acts through people who might "shake up" the church. Renewal involves risk, and therefore it requires leaders who are not afraid to permit things to happen that they cannot totally control if they discern that God may be behind it. Leaders cannot forget that the church belongs to God, to Jesus Christ, and that they are God's servants. Jesus guides, rules, and shepherds the church, because it belongs to him. If leaders obstruct God's plan and actions, the church will not be renewed, and they will be held responsible (see Ezekiel 34:1–10; John 10:12–13).

The church's history tells of many bishops, popes, and other ordained leaders who have "sparked" and led renewal. God gave them the vision and direction the church needed for reform or renewal, and they courageously responded in faith, often in the face of opposition. Some of these were mentioned in the last chapter, and this chapter will discuss more of them. Other leaders have been successful in recognizing and affirming the renewal that the Holy Spirit has stirred up through the charisms and callings given to the faithful and to movements in the church.

The responsibility of leadership is not easy, and that is why Christians must constantly pray for their leaders. We must pray that the Lord will give them the grace and wisdom they need to bring forth authentic renewal while keeping the church unified.

St. Athanasius and the Bishops Who Promoted the Ascetic Movement
After the condemnation of Montanism, one might have thought that the Catholic church was opposed to prophecy and other

charisms and to strict ascetic practices. These had been the central elements of the Montanist movement. However, the ascetic or monastic movement was based on a very strict life of self-denial and the manifestation of a variety of unique (and often extreme) charisms among the desert fathers and woman ascetics. Both these movements saw and presented themselves as a renewal of the Christian life as taught by Jesus, St. Paul, and other apostles and evangelists.

While there is no firm historical evidence of any bishop who came to the defense of the Montanists, there are many bishops who defended and promoted the ascetic movement. Beginning in the fourth century, these ecclesiastical patrons used their influence to foster the growth and acceptance of monasticism.

As mentioned previously, Athanasius, bishop of Alexandria, Egypt, from 328 to 373, was the most influential advocate of the ascetic movement, and the monks loved him as a father. His biography of Antony of Egypt led the church to recognize Antony as the founder of monasticism and, more importantly, to view the ascetic life as a truly Christian lifestyle. St. Athanasius saw this movement as a source of grace for the whole church because of the inspiration, prayers, and teaching (often in the form of pithy and enigmatic sayings) of the monks.

The monastic movement was an extreme response to the gospel, but for that very reason it became a seedbed for holiness and even for future church leaders. Some of history's greatest bishops and Christian teachers were formed, for a time, by the ascetic life of intense prayer, penance, and separation from normal society. These include Sts. Basil, Gregory of Nyssa, and Gregory of Nazianzen (the Cappadocian fathers), St. John Chrysostom, St. John Damascene, St. Martin of Tours, St.

Augustine of Hippo, and Pope St. Gregory the Great. This is not to mention the Father of Western Monasticism, St. Benedict, who was never a bishop nor (technically) a theologian.

In such a widespread and diverse movement, there were bound to be extremes and aberrations. The Messalians or Euchites ("praying people") believed that each person had a demon united with his or her soul that could only be expelled by concentrated and ceaseless prayer. They also thought that the ascetic life would provide them with a direct vision of the Blessed Trinity.[1] They saw little need for work: Prayer was the only necessary human activity. They were condemned by the Council of Ephesus in 431 but existed into the seventh century.

One extremist, St. Simeon Stylites, was perfectly orthodox in his beliefs and indeed was canonized, in spite of the peculiarity of his vocation. This fifth-century ascetic lived atop a stone pillar in the desert. He even gave rise to a new class of ascetics, the Stylites, who also lived atop pillars, were praised as holy men, and were consulted for advice and spiritual instruction.[2]

So the ascetic movement had its radical fringe and extremist tendencies, but history has shown it to be a tremendous contributor to the ongoing renewal of the Catholic church. Bishops generally were able to guide the movement in true and constructive directions, while occasionally condemning extreme groups who broke from the church's official teaching. Even authentic Catholic renewal movements will have their shortcomings and members or branches that fall into error and breach the unity of the church. What is more striking is how effectively most of the ascetic movement was integrated into the one church, both in its beginnings and as it developed over many centuries.

How was the monastic movement integrated into the church? It was the prototype for religious life: a life consecrated to God through vows to live in poverty, chaste celibacy, and obedience to the superiors of the particular religious community. Some male elders in the ascetic movement were ordained to the priesthood and even became bishops and popes.[3] Many of the ministries of the monks were beneficial to the whole church and to the culture, such as the copying of books and manuscripts before the printing press existed. The monastic movement also provided forms of prayer and liturgical music that were used outside of the monasteries. The monks also passed on wisdom to the wider church through their sayings and writings and the inspiration of their lives totally dedicated to God.

Truly the monastic-ascetic movement was a leaven of renewal for the entire church, and this was only possible because of the recognition, encouragement, and (at times) guidance of the church's bishops. As one author commented: "On reading the writings of the great bishops and monks of this early medieval period, what is especially striking is the affection and humanity of their relations, especially in the context of a violent and oppressive age."[4]

The Carolingian Era

The premise that the church cannot be renewed effectively without the support and approval of ecclesial authorities needs to be expanded in the Middle Ages to include the support and approval of Christian rulers, who often wielded powerful influence in the church. This is certainly true of Charlemagne, whose long reign as king and later as Holy Roman Emperor (768–814) marked the beginning of the era that bears the name *Carolingian*, derived from the Latin form of his name. The mottoes inscribed on his coins summarize the essence of his priorities: *religio christiani* (the Christian religion) and *renovatio Romani imperii* (renewal of the Roman Empire).

Charlemagne, like Constantine, saw the promotion and spread of the church as central to his mission. Much of what he did would be categorized under the headings of evangelization, education, and ecclesiastical organization and administration. Regarding education Charlemagne understood that, in order to practice the faith and abide by the moral law, one first had to know it. The British monk Alcuin (735–804) served as a minister of education under Charlemagne, seeking to spread knowledge of the faith. The rejuvenation of learning in this period has been called the Carolingian Renaissance.

The Benedictine monasteries were also renewed, led by the efforts of St. Benedict of Aniane (750–821). "In 779 he founded …at Aniane…a monastery which became the centre of an extended reform of all the French monastic houses."[5]

The tone that Charlemagne set encouraged the bishops to promote prayer and the renewal of the church. For example, Bishop Theodulf of Orleans supported Charlemagne's directives (called "capitularies") that every Christian be able to recite the Creed and the Our Father.

> The bishop added they must pray at least twice a day (morning and night), attend mass but do no work on Sunday, give shelter to the homeless, refrain from perjury and false testimony, be fair in business, and go to confession, where they must especially note their failure to avoid the eight vices, which Theodulf didactically listed for his priests. For the sal-

vation of souls, Bishop Theodulf particularly directed his priests to teach their parishioners and explain scripture to them. The capitularies had also stipulated frequent sermons in the vernacular language so every listener, whether literate in Latin or not, could understand.[6]

The Gregorian Reform

Pope St. Gregory VII, pope from 1073 to 1085, is best known for his conflict with the Holy Roman Emperor Henry IV over lay investiture and papal authority. Gregory reasserted papal authority over secular rulers in that struggle and in his famous bull of 1075, *Dictatus Papae.*

Pope Gregory was also a powerful force in renewing the church. In his writings he avoids the words *reformation* and *reform*, preferring to speak of his goal to renew (*renovare*) or to restore (*restaurare*) the church to its prior form and fervor.[7] One author notes:

> This was a period of turbulent conflicts, but also of ecclesial vitality: in the Church of that period we find hermits, canons regular, monks, hospitaller and military orders, each with their own particular features. The Holy See often intervened too: it confirmed, juridically approved, protected and promoted these charisms.
>
> The ecclesial reform movement of Gregory VII is explained in this light.[8]

With this papal encouragement many new forms of monastic and clerical life emerged, often drawing inspiration from the Acts of the Apostles.[9]

One important tool that Gregory employed to renew the church was the synod, a gathering of bishops and other clergy convened by the pope. In his Lenten synod of 1078, he "began his work for the reform and moral revival of the Church by issuing decrees against the simony and incontinence of the clergy."[10] Pope Gregory collaborated with the bishops at this synod on a plan for the *restauratio* (restoration) of the church. They addressed the question, "What makes true penance?" and devised an answer that emphasized the need for personal conversion.

So in spite of his reputation as a pope preoccupied with issues of papal authority and European politics,

> Gregory VII did not overlook pastoral concerns in the body of the church and personal reform among individual Christians.... He was less the 'founder' of medieval papal monarchy than its 'forerunner' and a more pastoral pope than the canon lawyers who would dominate the see of Peter in coming centuries.[11]

Innocent III and the Mendicant Movement

Pope Innocent III (pope 1198–1216) was a canon lawyer by training and, like Pope St. Gregory VII, an astute ecclesiastical politician who actually achieved, for a time, the reality of papal supremacy in all the spheres that Gregory VII had proclaimed. He was the first to call the pope "the Vicar [representative] of Christ" (not just of St. Peter), and his pontificate is generally recognized as "the climax of the medieval Papacy."[12]

Innocent III was never canonized, nor was he given the title "Great." I believe that his holiness and greatness have been denied or overlooked because of his success in asserting papal supremacy in the social and political spheres. Neglected is the great charity for which he was well loved, as in feeding thousands from the papal purse during a famine and founding the famous

Hospital of the Holy Spirit in Rome, which cared for all who came, regardless of their social status or ability to pay. But how can anyone overlook his leadership in the renewal of the church?

First, Innocent III called the most influential and successful ecumenical council of the Middle Ages, the Fourth Lateran Council (1215), which passed and effectively implemented numerous reform and renewal decrees, such as the requirement (still in force) of the reception of Holy Communion and the sacrament of penance at least annually (the "Easter duty"). Second, Pope Innocent approved the ministry and emerging order of Francis of Assisi. This was a bold step in faith, because other groups of "poor men" in recent memory had begun as loyal members of the church, received papal approval, and yet later became critical of the church and ended up being condemned as heretics or schismatics.

The Poor Men of Lyons, led by Peter Waldo (or Valdes), were approved by Pope Alexander III in 1179, with the caveat that as laypeople they could not present doctrinal preaching, only exhortations to conversion and virtue. The Waldensians caused many problems and were finally condemned by Alexander's successor, Lucius III, in 1184. The Waldensians and other poverty groups had grown increasingly critical of the church's affluence and of immoral clergy, and they drew people away from the Catholic church.[13]

Twenty-five years after the condemnation of the Waldensians, Francis and a ragged group of followers appeared before Pope Innocent III asking the same permission for which the Waldensians had asked: to live and preach gospel poverty. It is not surprising that most accounts report that Innocent sent Francis away unceremoniously at their first meeting. But Thomas of Celano, Francis' early biographer, reports a second interview, which is enshrined in a fresco in the upper church of the basilica of St. Francis of Assisi:

> [Innocent III] remembered a vision he had seen only a *few days earlier*, and *instructed by the Holy Spirit*, he now believed it would come true in this man [Francis]. *He saw in a dream* the Lateran basilica [the Pope's cathedral, the "head and mother" of all churches] almost ready to fall down. A religious man, *small and scorned*, was propping it up with his own bent back so it would not fall. "I'm sure," he said, "he is the one who will hold up Christ's Church by what he does and what he teaches!" Because of this the lord pope easily bowed to his [Francis'] request [the approval of his order and rule]; from then on, filled with devotion to God, he always loved *Christ's servant* with a special love.[14]

Pope Innocent III was responsive to the Holy Spirit in recognizing in St. Francis of Assisi a different spirit and attitude than was present in the Waldensians and other schismatic groups. Francis loved the church in spite of its weaknesses and sought only to renew her by living the gospel, especially the call to imitate Christ in his humility and poverty. Pope Innocent III and the popes who succeeded him were not so caught up in worldliness and politics, as some accuse, that they failed to discern and promote true holiness. Some accounts say that Innocent ordained Francis a deacon, but the one certain thing is that he gave Francis initial approval to live by the gospel standards he had presented.

Later, at Francis' request, a cardinal-protector, Hugolin (or Ugolino)—later Pope Gregory IX (1227–1241)—was assigned to guide the order as it grew. Cardinal Hugolin helped Francis develop the Franciscan rule, approved by Honorius III in 1223, and later as pope canonized St. Francis in 1228, St. Antony of Padua in 1232, and St. Dominic in 1234.

The approval and support of these popes allowed the charisms of Francis of Assisi, Dominic Guzman, Simon Stock, and others to result in a powerful renewal of the Catholic church. These examples demonstrate how the grace of renewal is intended to strengthen and build up the church, to make her a more luminous witness to the presence of Jesus and his Holy Spirit in the church.

A third way that Pope Innocent III promoted renewal was in his attempts to reconcile and bring back to the church renewal groups that had gone into schism. The pope was not interested in condemning those groups. As the representative of Christ, the Good Shepherd, he desired to bring them back into the fold.

It should be noted that even before Francis came to him, Innocent had approved other groups that had emerged out of the poverty movement, even though these groups were somewhat critical of the church and were in danger of going into schism. One of these was the Poor Lombards, led by Bernard Prim. A second group was the Poor Catholics, founded by a Spaniard, Durand of Huesca.

> In 1208, they went to Innocent III, promising him to obey their bishops and to preach only with their permission. They likewise agreed to receive the Sacraments from any priest with faculties to administer them and to stop discouraging the faithful from paying the tithes required by the Church. The Pope then permitted them to keep on with their way of life. They proposed to follow the Gospel counsels as if they were precepts, to despise gold and silver, and take no thought for

the morrow. The clerks gave themselves over to study and engaged in polemics with the heretics, and the laymen did manual labor. All wore the religious habit with sandals, kept two Lents a year, and said a certain number of Paters and Aves seven times daily at the canonical hours.

As the bishops, however, continued their opposition, the "Poor Catholics" were finally obliged a few years later to become absorbed in the Augustinian Order.[15]

Also the *Humiliati* in Lombardy (northern Italy) had established up to 150 communities in the Milan diocese alone by 1216. When they first appeared they were suspect because their ash-gray habits resembled those of the Waldensians and heretical Cathari. Nonetheless, Innocent III approved them in 1201, and they flourished.

Pope Innocent III clearly recognized, even before Francis came to him, that the Holy Spirit was raising up lovers of gospel poverty to renew the church. The risk that groups in this movement might fall into schism or heresy did not daunt him. He did not want to risk an even greater danger: stifling the Holy Spirit and the renewal of the church.

As a pastor Innocent III had to deal with the difficulties and challenges that these groups posed. At one point a group of Poor Catholics violated some of the agreements they had made when they were approved by the pope. The archbishop of Narbonne wrote to Innocent, desiring to excommunicate the group in his diocese. Showing true pastoral wisdom, Innocent III sent back two letters with the same courier: one addressed to the archbishop, and one addressed to Durand of Huesca, leader of the Poor Catholics.[16]

Of the archbishop Innocent urged patience, encouraging him to wait "up to the time the tree is known by its fruits." One of the agreements that the Poor Catholics had violated was to abandon the attire they had worn before their reconciliation with the church. Innocent encouraged the archbishop to tolerate this so long as Durand and his followers adhered to the substance of the Catholic faith.

Innocent thought like a theologian far ahead of his time in insisting that some pluralism in the church, especially in outward appearance, does not deform it. He compared the church with a queen who is "invested with vanity" as she stands at the right hand of Christ, her spouse. Though not in agreement with the Poor Catholics' contentious behavior, he urged tolerance, "so that we would follow the example of him who was weak for the weak, indeed, who became all things to all men so that all would attain to him who wishes all men to be saved and come to the knowledge of the truth (cf. 1 Cor. 9:22; 1 Timothy 2:4)."

The way Innocent weaves Scripture into the fabric of his letters attests to his knowledge of the sacred texts. His argument reflects his concern both for the church's unity and for the salvation of Durand and his followers. Innocent wants the archbishop to adopt a "spirit of leniency...since most men are called back more easily by earnest reminders than by threats, and several kind tokens of favor reform better than the harshness of discipline."

Although in the past, Innocent argues, perverse people were excommunicated at sword's point, now they are converted by "the warm embrace of communion." Using a medieval analogy, he says that the prudent surgeon first applies a stinging medication to a wound, but the cure is completed with a pleasant ointment. The archbishop is to be that skilled physician striving to cure his patient. This implies that the "patient," the straying Poor Catholics, is indeed ill but not malicious. The archbishop must give them the benefit of the doubt and consider their disobedience a matter of weakness or misunderstanding, not of outright rebellion.

Turning to his letter to Durand and the Poor Catholics, Innocent shows a much sterner face. He warns:

> You who owe more to our grace of favor are throwing it away, you are becoming very insolent toward these men [the bishops], to such an extent that you bring to the church certain Waldensian heretics, not yet reconciled to the unity of the Church, so that they share the consecrated body of the Lord with you.

This is the first of the archbishop's accusations against Durand: sharing communion with heretics. Innocent proceeds to list them all and to discuss what he expects the group to do. Turning to the question of their attire, Innocent points out that although the reign of God is not a matter of exterior but of interior appearance, their old habit has caused scandal. Innocent insists that they change it, as Durand has promised, "that just as in the interior habit, so also in your exterior habit, you show yourself to have been separated from the heretics."

Again, Innocent refers to Scripture, this time to Paul, to illustrate his point. The Poor Catholics should strive for those things that lead to peace and the edification of all. Just as Paul refused to eat meat if it scandalized his brother, so the Poor Catholics should change their attire, as they have agreed, so as not to scandalize their fellow Catholics.

As befits an address to a poorly educated class in a gospel-oriented movement, Innocent's language is easily comprehensible, and the letter is filled with Scriptural references and allusions. Innocent is firm in his admonitions and yet evidently solicitous of their needs.

Innocent III's years of experience in dealing with similar problems are certainly reflected in these two letters. It is possible to perceive in them his approach to the exercise of papal authority with regard to the poverty movement. He urged the bishops, while not denying their responsibility to act against deviance from Catholic doctrine and practice, to exercise tolerance and restraint in dealing with the failings of groups that were at least attempting to remain in full communion with the church. He reminded them that their goal was the reestablishment of this unity, which could more often be achieved by patience and good example than by persecution.

Innocent III was encouraging and supportive of groups within the poverty movement who sought communion with the church while not compromising any of the requirements of Catholic dogma and usage. This approach provides some of the reasons for Innocent's success in bringing the church closer to unity during his pontificate. It is also a powerful illustration of the proper pastoral use of authority to maintain the church's unity while seeking to promote renewal through a movement discerned as originating from the grace of God but needing guidance and, at times, correction. Many more recent popes have exhibited similar wisdom in reconciling groups with the Catholic church, such as Pope Benedicts XVI's efforts to welcome and receive Anglicans and others who desire to enter into full communion with the Catholic church.

The Catholic Reformation

The last chapter reviewed the power of personal charism of a number of saints of the Catholic Reformation—Ignatius of Loyola, Philip Neri, Teresa of Avila, and John of the Cross. As a result of their activity and that of many other ordinary people who responded wholeheartedly to extraordinary grace, the Catholic church was set on a new path of reform, and the spiritual lives of many were set ablaze. This chapter will consider the question: Could this have been accomplished without the cooperation, support, and leadership of the church's ordained leaders? What was the role of the bishops, cardinals, and popes in the reform and renewal of the Catholic church in the sixteenth century, and how important was that role?

Speaking in general terms, first, it is certain that the specific charisms and graces that came through Ignatius, Philip, Teresa, John, and many others would not have been brought into the mainstream of the church's life and have influenced so many had not the spiritualities and religious groups they spawned been approved by the bishops and the pope. The approval of Ignatius' order in 1540, the recognition of the Oratory movement and its canonical approval in 1575, and the establishment of the Discalced Carmelites as a distinct religious group within the Carmelite tradition all are specific ways that the pope and the bishops supported and advanced the church's renewal.

It must be said, second, that the corruption of the hierarchy and the abuses it perpetrated or ignored were a major cause of the crisis that resulted in the Protestant Reformation. Bishops and popes, as well as religious, laypeople, and other clergy, who were not living their faith vibrantly and were guilty of many sins, were also responsible for the dire need for reform and renewal. Indeed, they needed this reform and renewal in their own lives.

It should be noted that, in this period, church renewal can never be separated from church reform. Abuses and weaknesses were so entrenched and prevalent that correction of these problems was essential for any meaningful renewal to occur. Though we may distinguish between reform, renewal, and restoration, in reality these terms all point to the fact that the church requires purification and healing as well as strengthening and revitalization.

Here I will focus on a few examples of church leaders who responded to the grace of renewal in this period.

Pope Paul III

There is one pope who marks a turning point toward a serious process of reform and renewal. Pope Paul III, of the Farnese family, was "[i]n his personal habits...no great example of a reformed Pope, for he suffered from a numerous and avaricious family. But reformed or not, he was convinced by the urgent need to reform the Church from within. And his performance was courageous."[17]

Soon after becoming pope in October 1534, Paul began to unfold his plan of reform and renewal. His first step (in 1535) was to confer a cardinal's hat on Gaspar Contrarini, an eminent Venetian layman who was known for his desire to reform the church and enter into constructive dialogue with Protestants. In 1536 Paul III began to assemble a reform commission in Rome under Contrarini's leadership. This group in 1537 presented to the pope a very blunt and comprehensive statement of the most important reforms needed in the Catholic church, the *Consilium de Emendanda Ecclesia*. As the noted historian Ludwig Pastor declared, "the wounds had been laid bare, and now the remedy could be applied."[18]

Paul III was so pleased that even before the statement was completed, he raised three more members of the commission to the cardinalate: Carafa (later Pope Paul IV), Sadoleto, and the Englishman Reginald Pole. After the document was published, Luther had it translated into German and published it, with his own preface and notes, to demonstrate that he had been right about the need for reform in the Catholic church.

Pope Paul III saw the findings of his reform commission as the impetus he needed to convene, at last, the council of reform that had been so often discussed. The long delay had been due to debate over where to hold it and, most of all, fear on the part of previous popes that a reform council would undermine papal authority and possibly even be hijacked by Protestants. Paul III had the courage to convene the Council of Trent in 1545. His resolve was strengthened by the support of the Society of Jesus, which he had approved in 1540, and other emerging Catholic religious orders, both new and renewed.

Thanks to Pope Paul III, the momentum for reform and renewal of the Catholic church began to grow. He placed the papacy squarely in the center of the reform, leading the way. This is in stark contrast to the papacy of earlier years. Owen Chadwick observes "almost a different world" emerging:

> On the one side is a world of Italian Renaissance: gay, humane, corrupt, reasonably content with the old ways and the old abuses, still thinking of crusades against the Saracens when it thought of crusades at all, valuing the ascetic life deeply but regarding the ascetics as men to be admired rather than imitated by the world. On the other side is a world in earnest: seeking discipline and order, not only admiring the friars but wanting the Church to conform to the ascetic or puritan pattern, suspicious of nudes and pagan statues, fiercely struggling to diminish or eradicate the venality of church administration.

> The atmosphere of religious, moral, and intellectual life was being transformed. Bishops who had once been tranquil in their non-residence now issued circulars denouncing non-residence. Secretaries who once drafted the seamier documents of the indulgence traffic were now loud in denouncing the abuses of the indulgence. Humanists who once hired their pens to immoral literature were not ashamed to publish books of devotion.[19]

The pontificate of Paul III, which ended in 1549, was a turning point, a critical moment when the inclination to be satisfied with the past was overcome by an awareness that the church, or some part of it, needed to be taken in a new direction by the Holy Spirit. Of course, authentic reform and renewal is never merely a break from the past (we are not free to create a "new" church) but a return to the true tradition and identity of the church in a new and deeper way.

The popes of the sixteenth century were at a turning point in another way: Their ability to direct the church and effect reform and renewal was becoming more limited with the rise of nationalism. As Owen Chadwick put it,

> the States of Europe were restricting papal authority. To expect the Pope to reform the Church was to expect a miracle which he had little power to perform. He might give impetus to reform by example, or by influence, or by teaching; but the days were passing when he could command—supposing that he wished to command.[20]

With the political and worldly power of the papacy in decline, a situation that has continued to the present day, the popes had to reform and renew the church by other means, such as by example, moral influence, and teaching. This situation also highlighted the importance of working with and through the bishops. Pope Paul III, realizing the limitations of papal power, enlisted the bishops' help by calling the Council of Trent. (This realization perhaps led to the increased emphasis on the "collegiality" of the church's leaders, which was a focus of the Second Vatican Council.)

One of the bishops who exemplified the supportive reform bishop, dedicated to church renewal, was St. Charles Borromeo, archbishop of Milan from 1560 to 1584. A nephew of Pope Pius IV, the young Borromeo was an example of some of the worst abuses of the time, being made an archbishop with multiple sees at age twenty-one and a cardinal at age twenty-two. However, after undertaking the Spiritual Exercises of St. Ignatius of Loyola at age twenty-five, he adopted a life of self-denial and began to preach. As his reputation and stature as a reform bishop grew, he helped direct two commissions at the last session of the Council of Trent (1562–1563): on the implementation of the council's teaching and the production of a revised Catholic catechism incorporating that teaching.[21]

After the council Charles moved back to Milan and "was the new model of a Catholic bishop, constantly engaged in visiting his parishes," establishing seminaries, holding diocesan synods to implement the council's teaching, and establishing a diocesan religious order (the Oblates of St. Ambrose), an educational society serving 740 schools, and the Confraternity of Christian Doctrine to educate children in the faith.[22]

Pope Leo XIII

A final example of the influence of the leaders of the Catholic church in promoting church renewal prior to the twentieth century is the pontificate of Leo XIII (1878–1903). The two centuries prior to this were marked by the emergence of "Enlightenment" thought, which stressed the preeminence of reason in guiding human affairs. Ironically, it was also a period marked by violent revolutions in many of the same places where reason was being heralded, such as in France. Overall the period is often (rightly, in many respects) characterized as a time when the Catholic church was under siege.

The response of some popes, such as Leo's immediate predecessor, Pius IX, was primarily to uncover and condemn errors in the world that led to confusion regarding the truth and to political and social chaos. Widely publicized was Pope Pius IX's 1864 "Syllabus of Errors," which culminated in its last point: condemning as an error the proposition that the Catholic church must reconcile herself with "progress, liberalism, and modern civilization."[23]

One would need to undertake a thorough, careful study to understand and evaluate both the Enlightenment of the seventeenth through mid-nineteenth centuries and the teaching of Blessed Pope Pius IX. My purpose is simply to allude to some of the challenges faced by Leo XIII in the last quarter of the nineteenth century.

Pope Leo XIII has been both criticized and praised for taking what appears to be a moderate or middle-of-the-road stance toward the issues raised by the Enlightenment and the modern world. Diplomatically, he restored Vatican relations with many countries, most notably with Germany after its *Kulturkampf* (cultural war), which had been directed especially against Catholicism. Rather than disengaging the church from the world, Leo XIII spoke out boldly on social issues and on the rights and limitations of government. He is best known in this sphere for the first modern "social encyclical" (statement on social issues),

Rerum Novarum (1891), which emphasized the rights and dignity of workers.

In terms of scholarship, Leo's 1879 encyclical *Aeterni Patris* enjoined Catholics to study St. Thomas Aquinas as the "normative" teacher of our tradition, yet he also encouraged, in *Providentissimus Deus* (1893), the study of the Bible using new scholarly methods and approaches. These methods were fostered by the Pontifical Biblical Commission, which Leo founded in 1902. On the other hand, he declared Anglican orders to be invalid (1896) and in 1899 condemned a modernist heresy emerging from the United States, dubbed "Americanism." It may be said that he was responsible for a renewal of scholasticism and biblical studies.[24]

What is striking, though, about Pope Leo XIII is the breadth of his contributions and interests. I contend that Pope Leo XIII is, in this regard, a model or "template" for the modern papacy. In his approach to social issues, he prefigures Popes John XXIII, Paul VI, John Paul II, and Benedict XVI. And at the heart of this modern papacy is a concern for and commitment to reviving the spirituality of the church—that is, spiritual renewal.

The Oxford Dictionary of the Christian Church (second edition) lists some of Leo's contributions in the spiritual realm:

> Leo XIII promoted the spiritual life of the Church in many encyclicals dealing with the redemptive work of Christ, the Eucharist, and devotion to the B[lessed] V[irgin]M[ary] and the Rosary; and he sought to renew the spirit of St. Francis by modifying the rules of the Third Order in accordance with the requirements of his times. Following a revelation received by Mary von Droste-Vischering, religious of the Good Shepherd

of Angers, he consecrated the whole human race to the Sacred Heart of Jesus in the jubilee year 1900.[25]

This is a good summary, except for the omission (here and throughout the entire *Oxford Dictionary* article) of any mention of Pope Leo's emphasis on the Holy Spirit and his role in the renewal of the church. Pope Leo XIII authored the first modern encyclical letter on the Holy Spirit, *Divinum Illud Munus*, in 1897. In this work he "explicitly recommends to all Christians a devotion to the Spirit. He sees in it the efficacious and indispensable means of a renewal for contemporary society, for the family and for individuals…. Again he prescribed the celebration of the novena of Pentecost in all parish churches."[26]

In an earlier document, *Provida Matris Caritate*, Pope Leo had called the whole church to observe the church's original novena—the novena leading up to Pentecost—for a great outpouring of the Holy Spirit. And in response to a letter from Blessed Elena Guerra, foundress of the Oblate Sisters of the Holy Spirit, the pope, at his Mass on December 31, 1900, entrusted the new century to the Holy Spirit on behalf of the whole church.[27]

At her beatification on April 26, 1959, Blessed Pope John XXIII referred to Sister Elena as "the Apostle of the Holy Spirit" and stated: "Her message is always relevant. We are well aware, in fact, of the need for a continued effusion of the Holy Spirit, as of a new Pentecost which will renew the face of the earth."[28]

Here is another example of the charism of one of the church's ordinary members, Elena Guerra, affecting and being confirmed by members of the church's hierarchy, in this case two popes, Leo XIII and Blessed John XXIII, and through their influence sparking renewal in the universal church. The editors of a magazine article about Elena Guerra's correspondence with Pope Leo XIII add a note: "It is an interesting coincidence that also on the night of December 31, 1900, in Topeka, Kansas, Rev. Charles Parham prayed with Agnes Ozman to be baptized in the Holy Spirit—an occasion generally accepted as the beginning of the Pentecostal movement."[29]

Now that we have looked at historical examples of the role of personal charisms of individuals and the role of church leaders in the renewal of the church, it is fair to conclude that there is a significant pattern. That is, there is a "spiritual symbiosis" or complementarity between the charisms that God grants to individuals and the discernment, guidance, and support of those charisms by the church's leaders (as well as the exercise of the leaders' own unique gifts and roles in God's plan). Together these often bear the good fruit of ongoing and necessary renewal of the church. This is no more than a confirmation, through historical study, of the Pauline theology of how the various charisms given by the Holy Spirit work together for the growth and edification of the body of Christ.

Not all Catholic theologians and historians have reached this conclusion in their studies. In fact, in a major influential book published in 1950 (*Enthusiasm: A Chapter in the History of Religion with Special Reference to the XVII and XVIII Centuries*), Catholic theologian Father Ronald Knox concludes that the prevalent type of church renewal that he labels "enthusiasm" is actually divisive and dangerous, a deceptive trap to be avoided, at least from a Catholic perspective. Because of the influence of this book, or at least the widespread point of view that it represents, the next chapter will examine and evaluate Father Knox's criticism of the brand of renewal he labels "enthusiasm."

Enthusiasm *Revisited*

For many Catholics the phrase *church renewal* implies not only innovation or change in the church but also some type of religious emotion, feeling, or experience. This is not necessarily the case: Church renewal may be seen as a rational program or as the result of a particular divine grace that has nothing to do with any subjective revelation, experience, or encounter with God. Nonetheless there is a tendency for some to approach renewal in the church as something that gets people excited or "charged up" about God. It is seen as an appeal to the emotions, or the heart, that motivates people to change their lives and to change the church according to God's will and plan.

This latter concept of renewal is what Monsignor Ronald Knox studied in his 1950 book, *Enthusiasm*. The subtitle of the book, *A Chapter in the History of Religion with Special Reference to the XVII and XVIII Centuries,* indicates its focus.

"Enthusiasm" is a tendency that Knox finds in the primitive church and (in different forms) in other groups and movements thereafter. However, in his estimation it reaches its climax beginning in seventeenth-century England (with George Fox and his Society of Friends or "Quakers") and in France, with the Jansenists, Quietists, and other groups such as the "French Prophets" (the *Camisards*) and the so-called Convulsionaries of Saint-Medard. In the eighteenth century an even greater height of "enthusiasm" was reached with the continental Moravian tradition and, finally, with the British evangelical revival, which, in Knox's view, finds its purest expression in John Wesley and the Methodists. As eminent Roman Catholic church historian Christopher Dawson explains: "The real subject of Mgr. Knox's book is enthusiasm in the classical eighteenth-century sense of the word, that is to say, a kind of unbridled religious emotionalism which expresses itself in the orgies of revivalism and in the moral disorders of antinomianism."[1]

Ronald Knox's interest in this phenomenon is understandable. He was raised in a "low church" Anglican family; his father was an Anglican priest and later a bishop. He lived in a nation heavily influenced by Methodism and the evangelical revival. After an intense intellectual struggle and participation in an extremely Anglo-Catholic wing of the Church of England, Ronald Knox decided to join the Catholic church and began to write apologetic works in defense of Roman Catholicism. Part of that defense was to be a denunciation of "enthusiasm," which he saw as the heart of evangelical Christianity. He claimed that although this evangelical revival awakened eighteenth-century England from its religious apathy, it failed in its long-term effects:

> Religion became identified in the popular mind with a series
> of moods, in which the worshipper, disposed thereto by all the

arts of the revivalist, relished the flavors of spiritual peace. You needed neither a theology nor a liturgy; you did not take the strain of intellectual inquiry, nor associate yourself whole-heartedly with any historic tradition of worship. You floated, safely enough, on the little raft of your own faith, eagerly throwing out the lifeline to such drowning neighbors as were ready to catch it; meanwhile the ship was foundering.

It is this by-passing of an historic tradition in favor of a personal experience that has created the modern religious situation in England, and to some extent in the English-speaking world.[2]

In the book's dedication (to Evelyn Waugh), Knox explains that he has been writing "the Book" for over thirty years, adding to it and revising it every year. He explains that he set out to write "a broadside, a trumpet-blast, an end of controversy," to show "what happens inevitably if once the principle of Catholic unity is lost."[3]

This is noteworthy; all of the historical examples given in the book are groups that either divided from their "parent church" (whether Catholic, Anglican, or other) or had been condemned by that church. It is not surprising that Knox, in the book's first paragraph, describes enthusiasm as a "recurrent situation in Church history—using the word 'church' in the widest sense—where an excess of charity threatens unity."

What does Knox mean by an "excess of charity"? He continues, not with a definition but with a description of this historical recurrence: "You have a clique, an *élite*, of Christian men and (more importantly) women, who are trying to live a less worldly life than their neighbors; to be more attentive to the guidance (directly felt, they would tell you) of the Holy Spirit. More and more, by a kind of fatality, you see them draw apart from their co-religionists." Then, after an escalating series of suspicions, criticisms, and accusations, there is a break of the "clique" from its parent church body: "condemnation or secession, what difference does it make? A fresh name has been added to the list of Christianities."[4]

Knox's main criticism of the tendency that he calls enthusiasm boils down to this: It is divisive, violating the central Catholic value and principle of unity. His secondary criticism is that enthusiasm is based on religious experience or emotion, not on reason nor on faith. For Knox experience is not a reliable ground for accepting any opinion about God or the church because it is purely subjective and thus might be an illusion. He wrote in his autobiography:

> [M]y own "experience" of Christianity might, for all I knew, be an illusion—how much more the alleged "experience" of other people?.... "Authority" must mean more than the results of a scientific induction; it must be something *sui generis*, with a corresponding faculty (of faith), equally *sui generis*, to apprehend its deliveries....
>
> ...I [came to believe] that the authority of an infallible Church was necessary to the confident preaching of any Christian doctrine.[5]

He alludes here to the reason for his own conversion to Roman Catholicism: his acceptance of the authority of the Catholic church based on faith in what it teaches. Apparently, for Knox, faith in the truth claims of an institution, unlike religious experience, is not subjective and cannot be an illusion. The reality is that whatever leads a person to accept God as real and important, or a religious body as true, in an exclusive sense, is something that is personal or personally compelling, whether it be called faith, reason, or experience.

Ronald Knox wants to exclude religious experience as a way of coming to the truth. In a letter dated October 5, 1931, to Arnold Lunn, who converted to Catholicism after an extended correspondence with Knox, Knox wrote:

> [T]o me all this modern talk about religious experience is cant; that is to say, when it is used for apologetic purposes. If a man professes to accept any religious doctrine only or chiefly on that ground, claiming that he or any other man has "verified" it by "experience,"...I say that is cant, and mischievous cant.[6]

"Ultrasupernaturalism"

Knox coins a word for the tendency of the religious "enthusiast" who has fallen into this error of divisiveness based on religious experience or emotion. He calls it "ultrasupernaturalism." Knox says that it is based on a false theological position: that a person can be freed completely from the weakness of human nature and live solely by grace. Instead of perfecting or elevating human nature, grace replaces nature. It is literally true, in this ultrasupernaturalist view, that by the grace of God a person becomes a totally "new creation" (2 Corinthians 5:17), that the former "worldly" nature passes away completely and is replaced by a new "spiritual" nature. This is an exaggeration of the traditional Catholic belief that the grace of Christ, given especially in baptism and the other sacraments, has cleansed the baptized from original sin and set him or her free from many of its effects.

Second, the advent of this total transformation of the person leads the ultrasupernaturalist to recognize a new standard of what is normative for a Christian's commitment and moral life. As Knox says, he now "expects more evident result from the grace of God than we others."[7] The only acceptable standard for the Christian is total commitment to Christ and a life of uncompromising virtue and moral purity. Knox terms this attitude "rigorism" and calls attention to the paradox that this tendency sometimes breeds its opposite, "antinomianism," which is a belief that "actions which bring damnation to the worldlings may be inculpable in the children of light."[8]

The third characteristic of ultrasupernaturalism that Knox proposes is an emphasis upon direct, personal access to God. Religion becomes primarily an "affair of the heart," and this inward orientation consequently takes precedence over outward forms of worship and ordinances, such as sacraments. These are not necessarily dispensed with but are normally considered to be less important than the personal approach of the individual to God.

This tendency has two distinct variations. In one form it values "[a]n inward experience of peace and joy [that] is both the assurance which the soul craves for and its characteristic prayer-attitude."[9] Consolations, the tangible experiences of God's presence and love, are to be expected and enjoyed.

The other variation also emphasizes a direct, personal relationship with God but without expecting any sensible experience of his favor or presence. In fact, consolations or any positive emotions in prayer are shunned as being obstacles to loving God for his own sake.[10]

In the last chapter of *Enthusiasm*, Knox labels these tendencies "evangelical enthusiasm" and "mystical enthusiasm." He also contrasts these tendencies when he discusses the different historical "enthusiastic" movements, a discussion that constitutes the largest portion of his book. Some movements draw the conclusion that since our relationship with God is so immediate, we can expect his daily guidance and revelation through direct inspiration. Certainly the traditional Christian relies on God's guidance, but for the ultrasupernaturalist this guidance is direct and pervasive. George Fox's doctrine of the "inner light" is the best-known example of this belief.[11]

Exaggerated reliance upon the direct guidance of God results in the fourth characteristic of ultrasupernaturalism, the distrust of human reason and the intellect. This is also a corollary of the belief that grace replaces nature, because the truly spiritual man need not be directed by purely human faculties, such as the mind, which have been fatally impaired by the Fall. Least of all can these "worldly" faculties be employed to discern religious truth.[12] Knox notes the result of this reasoning:

> In matters of abstract theology the discipline of the intellect is replaced by a blind act of faith. In matters of practical deliberation, some sentiment of inner conviction, or some external "sign" indicative of the Divine will, claims priority over all considerations of common prudence.[13]

Specifically, human prudence is replaced either by direct divine inspiration (for example, the inner light), by prophetic messages or signs, or by the drawing of lots, trusting that God will determine the outcome. Certainly the traditional Christian does not deny that God sometimes guides Christians by extraordinary means such as these, but he cannot concur with the ultrasupernaturalist that these are the primary, normal ways a Christian's life is directed and religious truth revealed. They do not replace human reason, discernment by a community, or the authoritative teaching of a church.[14]

A fifth common trait of the ultrasupernaturalist is the expectation of miracles and other tangible signs of God's activity in the world. The "evangelical enthusiast" normally expects some "sensational accompaniments" to the process of conversion and looks for external signs, such as "odd physical manifestations," as testimony to God's power and presence.[15] Although such signs are prone to conflicting or erroneous interpretations, they continue to be avidly sought after by many ultrasupernaturalists.

A sixth trait of the ultrasupernaturalist is a reaction against institutionalized religion and the longing for a "theocracy"—a society in which righteous believers rule. All too often the visible institution of the church seems to the ultrasupernaturalist to have slipped into a regrettable alliance with the world. Knox repeatedly uses the phrase "the church has unchurched herself" to describe this tendency. The ultrasupernaturalist suspects that the secular society and government either control the church directly or have so influenced it that it is no longer an effectively witnessing, vibrant Christian body. As a result, "Always the enthusiast hankers after a theocracy, in which the anomalies of the present situation will be done away, and the righteous bear rule openly."[16]

An extreme form of this theology is the doctrine, originated by Wycliffe and Hus, that "dominion is founded on grace."[17] This means that in God's eyes only true Christians, and not the ungodly, have any right to rule or to possess any legal rights whatsoever. But practically speaking, since an effective theocracy has proven almost impossible to achieve on the level of a nation or state, it is common for ultrasupernaturalist groups to separate themselves geographically from the broader society in order to establish their own miniature theocracies—small utopian societies.[18]

Finally, the last two common characteristics of ultrasupernaturalism that Knox mentions are not essential to this phenomenon "but are not seldom its concomitants": "One of these is a conviction that the Second Coming of our Lord is shortly to be expected. Another is ecstasy; under which heading I include a mass of abnormal phenomena, the by-products, it would seem, of prophecy, or sometimes of 'convincement.'" These "abnormal phenomena" include, for Knox, glossolalia (that is, "speaking in tongues"), trances, and protracted convulsive movements of the entire body.[19]

In summary, Ronald Knox claims that the ultrasupernaturalist or religious enthusiast is guilty of an exaggeration of valid Christian doctrine or practice. As Knox explains, "traditional Christianity is a balance of doctrines, and not merely of doctrines but of emphases. You must not exaggerate in either [or any] direction, or the balance is disturbed."[20]

For Monsignor Knox Catholicism is balanced and reasonable, while the exaggerations of the religious enthusiast are not. Hence enthusiasm is, for Knox, an enemy of Christianity.

The effects of enthusiasm may vary according to how extreme the exaggerations are or the impact they have in the particular historical situation in which they occur. Sometimes religious enthusiasm might appear as just some unusual tendencies or viewpoints in a person, group, or movement in the church. Or it may lead to serious tension or confrontations among Christians or between the individual (or group) and the leaders of the church—whether local (priest, pastor, or bishop), national, or international (the pope or Vatican congregations). It may result in schism and the formation of new, independent Christian bodies.

Here I have been presenting Ronald Knox's perspective, which is clearly suspicious and critical of these tendencies that he considers divisive and erroneous. He does not see anything but danger in "religious experience," which is a component of ultrasupernaturalism. This, he believes, is simply not Catholic—not part of the Catholic church's doctrine and perspective. It is even, to some extent, anti-Catholic in Knox's view.

Early Examples of Enthusiasm

Knox draws these conclusions from his study of selected movements, groups, and individuals in the history of Christianity. He begins with St. Paul's correspondence with the church in Corinth around AD 57. This correspondence is particularly important because it is part of Sacred Scripture: God's revelation that is the foundation of Catholic belief and doctrine. Knox finds in Paul's Letters to the Corinthians some examples of problems that are common in enthusiastic groups and movements.

First, the community fell into schism over the issue of leadership and perhaps over who had the correct interpretation of Paul's doctrine. Internal schism is a common pitfall of enthusiastic movements, especially when a movement that is held together by the influence of one dominating individual confronts a crisis, such as the leader's death, withdrawal, or loss of ascendancy in the group.[21]

Another problem among the Corinthians was antinomianism, the belief that the gospel dispensation of grace frees one from observance of the moral law. Some of them, for example, apparently interpreted Paul's teaching on the limitation of the Mosaic Law to be a rejection of its standard for sexual morality, since they openly tolerated a clearly immoral situation in their midst. St. Paul affirms that the Mosaic Law is by no means abolished.[22]

Other indications of enthusiasm Knox mentions include a hint of rigorism among those Corinthians who wanted to abolish marriage and in St. Paul's warning about "unwholesome pre-occupation" with the charismatic gifts of prophecy and speaking in tongues. The Corinthians were evidently exercising these gifts in such a way that the greatest gift, charity, was violated or devalued. Knox's main point is that the early church was no utopia, and it possessed a great many symptoms of enthusiasm, which St. Paul strove to correct, not without a great deal of pain and difficulty.[23]

THE MONTANISTS

Montanism was a late second-century movement within Christianity that originated with the presbyter Montanus in Phrygia, a region of Asia Minor. One permanent contribution that the Montanists made to the vocabulary of enthusiasm was the distinction between the "carnal" and the "spiritual" Christian.[24] The followers of Montanus and the believers in his prophecies considered themselves the true, "spiritual" Christians because they held a more rigorous moral standard than the average Christian of their time and because they experienced ecstatic prophecy, which they interpreted as the sign of the inauguration of a new era of the Holy Spirit.[25]

Knox discounts the validity of Montanist prophecy, primarily because it was delivered by a prophet in an ecstatic state, for which he finds no precedent. Moreover, Knox is especially critical of Montanism's chief theologian, Tertullian, for trying to "stampede the Church into greater severity, when she had not forgotten how to be severe." He accuses Tertullian of contentiousness and of fabricating issues to the detriment of the Church's unity, "and to that extent...Montanism is less worthy of respect than most of the enthusiastic sects which have followed its example, and borrowed its language."[26]

Although Knox claims that his purpose is not to judge the movements he studies,[27] he does not hesitate to conclude, "The history of Montanism is not to be read as that of a great spiritual revival, maligned by its enemies. It is that of a naked fanaticism."[28]

THE DONATISTS

While "the rigorism of the Montanists," Knox says, "has something of the air of an afterthought," rigorism on a single point of doctrine was the chief cause of the Donatists' division from the church. Like many other enthusiastic movements, Donatism based its claim that it was the true church upon the belief that it was the only pure or holy church. It disregarded other aspects of the true church that are equally important, such as catholicity, apostolicity, and oneness, qualities that it possessed, at best, in a questionable or obscure sense of these terms.[29]

Donatism claimed to be the pure or holy church because of its severity toward *traditores*, those who had surrendered sacred books (especially the Bible) to persecuting government authorities. This led the Donatists into a "frankly charismatic view of the ministry,"[30] because they claimed that a bishop who had been a traditor forfeited the right to consecrate other bishops and that traditor priests had also lost their sacramental powers. According to their view, "the validity of a Sacrament depends on the worthiness of the minister" and not upon an irrevocable sacramental grace from God.[31]

Other exaggerated characteristics of Donatism included its exaltation of martyrdom and its rigorism in moral matters.[32] But

Knox views the central issue as the Donatists' denial of the possibility of a *traditor* being forgiven and continuing as a valid minister of the church. This leads him to question whether Donatism is truly an enthusiastic movement, since its schism appears to have sprung from a clear-cut issue of church discipline. Knox's answer to this question sheds light on his understanding of enthusiasm:

> The enthusiastic movements we propose to examine form a separate group of phenomena which can be distinguished from ordinary heresy (which springs from doctrinal disagreement) and from ordinary schism (which is the defection of a nation or of a local Church from the general body of Christendom). It may be asked here, whether Donatism should not have found its place among the schisms properly so-called, as a local defection of the African province. But... Donatism is not the child of an administrative disagreement, or of an historical accident; it is a protest of the rigorist against a supposed betrayal of the Christian conscience, and as such it has been allowed to figure in these pages.[33]

Knox's inclusion of Donatism as an enthusiastic movement demonstrates that his definition of enthusiasm is not limited to a particular form or type of exaggeration of Christian doctrine or discipline. Even a rather conservative reaction, such as Donatism's protest against the alleged laxity of the church in dealing with traditores, qualifies as a form of enthusiasm.

THE WALDENSIANS AND THE CATHARISTS

Knox's narrative then advances nearly a thousand years as he analyses two medieval movements: the Waldensians and the

Catharists. Both were concerned with restoring a gospel standard of simplicity to the life of the church, a reform that was undoubtedly needed. The Waldensians, named after their founder, Peter Waldo (or Valdes) of Lyons, wanted not only to live evangelical poverty but to proclaim this vocation publicly. In 1179 Pope Alexander III officially granted the Waldensian laymen permission to preach "on condition that they did not go about preaching except at the request of the local clergy."[34] The failure of some of them to follow this directive led to their condemnation by Pope Lucius III in 1184.

Knox is sympathetic to the Waldensians, comparing them favorably with the early Methodists in their desire to remain part of the church. But they also resemble the Wesleyans in the factors that eventually divided both movements from their parent churches: lay preaching and ordination.[35] For the most part their doctrine was Catholic, although they rejected infant baptism[36] and, like the Donatists, denied the validity of any sacramental activity of an unworthy minister.[37] They expected their priests to live strict, evangelical poverty.

In spite of their good intentions, Knox views the Waldensians' secession from the church as inevitable. He explains:

> It had never been their intention to set up a separate Church, any more than it was Wesley's intention, during his lifetime, to secede from Anglicanism. To be a leaven within the lump, to be an enclave of holiness within the corrupt body of Christendom, was the aim of either movement. But the logic of the facts was against them. The enthusiast always begins by trying to form a church within the Church, always ends up finding himself committed to sectarian opposition.[38]

Unlike the Waldensians, the Catharists held heretical dualistic doctrines (such as denial of the Incarnation) and were militantly opposed to the Roman Catholic Church. They established their own hierarchy in southern France, in opposition to the Catholic hierarchy, and, in keeping with their dualistic doctrine, denied the efficacy of all the Catholic sacraments.[39] They did retain one sacrament, the *consolamentum*, which "took the form of a confirmation, was credited with the effects of baptism, and replaced extreme unction [it was usually conferred at death]." The Catharists recognized two primary levels of sanctity among their members, that of the Believers (*Credentes*) and that of the Perfect (*Perfecti*), who had received the *consolamentum* and were judged to be paradigms of virtue.[40]

Throughout *Enthusiasm* Knox frequently charges those who claim to be perfect with antinomianism, the belief that they are no longer bound by any moral law. The Catharist Perfecti do not escape this accusation:

> But it is perhaps not unreasonable to suspect that the Cathari may have come to think of themselves as superior to all temptations of the flesh, and neglected, with unfortunate results, the conventions by which less hardy souls fortify their modesty.… In a word, the *Perfecti* were anticipating, by nearly seven centuries, the behavior of the Perfectionists.[41]

Knox conjectures that the dualism of the Perfecti led them to view the body's activities as spiritually inconsequential, so that sins of the "flesh" became meaningless to them, but he produces little evidence to support this claim. He is on safer ground when he proposes that antinomianism is a general tendency of the enthusiast, that "this deliberate flirting with the occasions of sin, in the belief that you are too holy to apprehend any danger from them, is a trick of the enthusiast."[42]

After so many examples of movements that have ended in schism and in extremes of belief and practice, it is reasonable to ask whether Knox believes that any movements with "enthusiastic" or "rigorist" tendencies have avoided these divisions or extremes. He does mention at least one group that succeeded in preaching and living the gospel radically within the framework of the institutional church—St. Francis of Assisi and his followers. However, his treatment of them is very brief,[43] and he predictably devotes greater attention to the stream of Franciscanism that ended in schism, the *Fraticelli* or spiritual Franciscans. They believed that "the Church had unchurched herself when she turned her back on poverty,"[44] which means that they desired a more radical interpretation and practice of evangelical poverty than the church and their fellow Franciscans were able to accept. Many of them also accepted the millenarian speculations authored by Abbot Joachim of Fiore. Knox thus demonstrates that a single movement, such as the poverty movement, can produce both "enthusiasts" who secede from their parent church and "saints" who remain within it.[45]

Some additional tendencies that Knox perceives in connection with these medieval heresies include the belief that the only true church is the "invisible church" of those predestined to be saved. Both Hus and Wycliffe held that "for the enthusiast, there is only one Church, a Church 'invisible.'"[46] Knox also observes that enthusiastic movements tend to attract the "plain man," usually of the lower middle class, rather than the intellectual or the financially stable and well-off. There are numerous exceptions to this, of course, such as Wycliffe and Wesley, who both had university educations. Paradoxically, though, men such as these were often the most outspoken critics of institutions of higher learning. They tended to deny the value of this training and identified themselves with the poorer and less educated classes.[47]

The Anabaptists

Next Knox advances to the Reformation period, focusing on the Anabaptist movement. He examines its origins and finds that a number of Anabaptist beliefs and practices were passed on to it from medieval heretical groups. Although generally he believes that "the enthusiastic tendency is one which recurs, as it were, by spontaneous generation, throughout the history of the Church,"[48] there are cases such as this in which enthusiastic movements have adopted certain beliefs and emphases from earlier groups and movements. The Anabaptists' doctrine of a spiritual church, the belief that "dominion is founded on grace" (Wycliffe), and the rejection of infant baptism and the doctrine of the Incarnation (Catharists) are proposed as examples. A number of Anabaptists also held the doctrine of perfectionism, which sometimes led to antinomianism.[49]

The Anabaptists also believed strongly in theocracy, the rule of spiritual men, which divided them from the majority of Protestant Reformers, who were willing to compromise and work with the secular state. Knox contends: "The true enthusiast can only be at home under a theocracy, with an accredited prophet as its visible head; any other form of government, because its sanctions depend on the natural order, is not merely inadequate, but evil."[50]

The incredible atrocities of the Anabaptist theocracy at Münster are, for Knox, a perpetual warning against the extremism possible in any attempt to establish the spiritual kingdom on earth. Although most Anabaptists thoroughly rejected the excesses of Münster, such as polygamy and even "free sex," the association of Münster's leader, John of Leiden, with Anabaptism discredited the movement as a whole. More commonly characteristic of Anabaptist theocratic experiments were small groups with a rigidly scheduled life, a strict code of morals, and a healthy exercise of discipline over the young.[51]

Besides the issue of theocracy, the Anabaptists also disagreed with Luther and the Reformers on the interpretation of the Bible. Luther gradually withdrew from the initial Protestant position that the Bible could always be interpreted correctly by the individual Christian, to the view that the rule of faith required the interpretation of the Bible by proper scholarship, that is, "Scripture as interpreted by Luther, and Calvin, and Zwingli, and Beza, and Knox—by the pundits."[52] But "[t]o the enthusiast, the Bible is infallible when interpreted by an inspired person."[53] Since the Anabaptists believed that God directly inspires each true Christian, there was no need for an authoritative interpreter of Scripture.

This, of course, accounts for the extremes of biblical interpretation in Anabaptism, which resulted in perfectionism, chiliasm, and the like as well as pacifism, the refusal to swear oaths, and sharing goods in common (see Acts 2:44–45). Knox concludes that the chief historical importance of Anabaptism is in "the recoil of official Protestantism from the very notion or mention of enthusiasm."[54]

The Anabaptists' conception of direct inspiration found its formal expression in George Fox's doctrine of the "inner light."[55]

Knox describes Quakerism in terms of a specification and further formulation of Anabaptist principles. Fox accepted the already rigorous moral standards of his day and "grafted on one or two oddities of behaviour," such as the refusal to swear oaths or to remove one's hat when custom called for it. Knox traces these practices back to Anabaptist customs or culture.[56]

Like the Anabaptists, Fox repudiated the notion of a visible church and sacraments and held to the Anabaptist view of scriptural interpretation by the direct inspiration of any believer.[57] But for Fox the ultimate authority was not Scripture but the direct guidance of the believer through the "inner light." The problem with this principle is that there is no objective standard of discernment to which the Quaker could appeal when conflicting guidance was received by different parties or when the inspiration received by one party seemed incorrect. Hypothetically, there is no way that a Quaker, even Fox, could gainsay the validity of guidance given to another individual by the "inner light."

The most striking illustration of this was the case of James Nayler, who was proclaimed by a group of Quakers led by Martha Simmonds to be a second incarnation of Christ. Although Nayler did not believe this and desired to remain loyal to Fox, he was afraid to deny the "inner light" of those who acclaimed him divine, for fear of opposing God. The doctrinal weaknesses of Quakerism finally caused it to succumb to the pervasive deism of its day, and today the Quakers retain few of the distinctively Christian beliefs that were held and proclaimed by George Fox.[58]

Jansenism and Quietism

In the first chapter of *Enthusiasm*, Knox writes: "[B]oth Jansenism and Quietism reproduce some features of the tendency we have been discussing. This needs to be said with caution, for neither movement will fit into the canvas of enthusiasm as we have delineated it."[59]

Indeed, Christopher Dawson finds no justification for the inclusion of Jansenism and Quietism in Knox's study, because they "did not consist in an unleashing of the forces of enthusiasm, but in the drying up of the great movement of Catholic mysticism which was the glory of the seventeenth century." Rather than exemplifying the "excess of charity," which for Knox characterizes enthusiasm, Dawson can only discern in these movements "an excess of animosity and hatred."[60]

Since neither of these movements fits the pattern of enthusiasm that Knox has established to this point, one may well ask why he treats them at length and how they advance his theory. The most marked attribute of Jansenism is its stern moral rigorism, which Knox labels "Puritanism...abstinence from acute pleasures and from careless behaviour on the grounds that such things are sinful."[61] Knox also provides an excellent summary of Jansenist teaching:

> That very few people go to heaven, and those only by a catastrophic exercise of God's mercy; that the *honnêtes gens* we come across are mostly reprobate,...that the chances are against your being one of the few elect, unless your life is heroically given to God as few people's lives are; that you must therefore give the world, and worldly people, a wide berth, for fear of acquiescing in their standards; that you must scrutinize all your motives carefully, to make sure that even your generous actions are dictated by love of God,...that in cases of doubt you must never give yourself the benefit of the doubt, but choose the course which is certainly inculpable; that if you

> fall into sin, you should make satisfaction for it by abstaining
> for a time from Communion, even when absolution has been
> granted; that such abstinence from Communion is sometimes
> a useful discipline, to be practiced with the advice of an
> enlightened director—that is the teaching of Port Royal; such
> is its genius.[62]

This teaching was the result of exaggeration of St. Augustine's theology of grace, which set the Jansenists in opposition to the more
moderate teaching and discipline of the church, especially that of
the Jesuits. The Jansenists' fault, Knox explains, was to abandon
Christian tradition in an attempt to approach Christianity *de novo*,
as the Reformers did, "replacing, however, the uninterpreted
Bible by an uninterpreted St. Augustine."[63]

As a consequence of the opposition they faced in the church,
and in order to isolate themselves from the "poisonous" influence
of worldly thought, the Jansenists turned their attention inward.
Although they never formally separated from the Catholic
church, Knox believes that they identified themselves either
explicitly or unconsciously with the "invisible Church," since
they believed that only they were preserving the true teaching of
the church.

Like Jansenism, Quietism was a Catholic movement that flourished in France, between 1650 and 1750, until it was finally condemned by the church. This, however, is about as far as the sim-
ilarity between the movements extends; in fact, they generally
opposed each other.[64] Jansenism bore some characteristics of
evangelical enthusiasm; Quietism is the epitome of mystical
enthusiasm. While the Jansenist, concerned with who was predestined, expected some sensible signs of being in God's grace, to

the Quietist a person's own salvation was to be a matter of complete indifference, and consolation in prayer or any attention to feeling was considered an imperfection. God was to be worshipped solely for his own sake. This was the Quietist notion of "disinterested love."[65]

Like the Jansenists, the Quietists came into open conflict with the Jesuits, but not over the issue of lax morality. Their disagreement concerned prayer. They had little regard for Jesuit meditation, even reflection on the mysteries of Christ's life, because they considered the contemplative "prayer of simple regard" as the ideal form of prayer.[66] Human effort was vain, because all is accomplished by God's grace. Knox comments on this doctrine:

> What lies at the root of the Quietist error? In the last analysis, a kind of ultra-supernaturalism.... [T]he Quietist wants to do away with human effort as such so as to give God the whole right of spiritual initiative. Primarily in his prayer; but ideally—why not?—in every other department of life. He is not content that grace should perfect the work of nature.... God alone must do everything; we cannot even co-operate with him, only allow him to operate in us, and forget that he even allows us to allow him.[67]

Knox argues that the Quietists encountered opposition because "they were trying to make good their position as ultra-mystics, when mysticism itself had not achieved a secure foothold."[68] But the Quietists—Gagliardi, Malaval, and especially Molinos and Madame Guyon—were not condemned because their timing was inopportune but because of certain "false emphases" inherent in their teaching. Knox explains their approach:

The more startling utterances of the mystical writers are sin-
gled out for our attention, and their implications are over-
stressed. Moreover, there is a tendency to exalt contemplative prayer as if it were the only exercise of the human spirit
really pleasing to God, really efficacious in promoting man's
salvation.[69]

The Quietists, as a movement, did not secede from the Roman
Catholic Church, possibly only because their chief ecclesiastical
proponent, Archbishop Fénelon, submitted to the church's judgment and discipline.[70] Thus Quietism remains a warning against
the excesses of mystical illuminism. It is also a source of some
hope that potentially schismatic movements of enthusiasm can be
dealt with and corrected within the church, if their leaders are
willing to accept the church's guidance and discipline.

The Camisards and the Convulsionaries
Two more manifestly enthusiastic movements arose in France
after Jansenism and Quietism. The first of these, appearing in the
late seventeenth century, was the movement of the French
Prophets or Camisards.

When the Edict of Nantes was repealed in 1685, the French
Huguenots were prone to excesses such as apocalypticism. A certain M. du Serre began to train a group of children in a style of
prophetic utterance that was induced and accompanied by violent physical manifestations. "The prophet beat his head with his
hands for some time, then fell down on his back; his stomach and
throat swelled up and he remained speechless for some minutes,
after which he broke out into utterance."[71]

Knox remarks that there were also "more highly colored
accounts." Adults in the movement later prophesied in this way

as well and sometimes relied on their prophecies to decide issues as serious as whether war prisoners should be slain or allowed to live. Knox concludes: "That is the worst of it; the ultrasupernaturalist faced with a moral problem believes that the solution is given to him directly by the voice of God, and from that arbitrament there is no appeal."[72]

Extremities such as this caused the Camisards to be exiled from France. They went to Germany, where, according to Knox, they may have "helped to arouse the spirit of enthusiasm which gave birth to the Moravian brethren and so, indirectly, to the Methodist movement in our own country."[73] Some Camisards also went directly to England, where they were welcomed at first as victims of unjust religious persecution. But the British were ultimately no more tolerant than the French when the Camisards began to prophesy against the clergy of the Church of England and to predict the destruction of London.[74] Their only major success in England was the conversion of Quaker Ann Lee, who later founded the Shakers in America.[75]

The second of the movements marked by evident external manifestations of enthusiasm was an outgrowth of Jansenism commonly known as the Convulsionaries of St. Médard. Its brief history began in 1728 with a healing at the tomb of a reputedly holy Jansenist, François de Pâris.[76] Two hundred alleged cures and miracles occurred at the cemetery of St. Médard between 1728 and 1731, which resulted in the site's becoming a noted pilgrimage center.

Knox conjectures that a combination of political events and the approach of a centenary of Jesus' death (1733) brought about an "apocalyptic atmosphere that created the convulsions."[77] Those who flocked to the cemetery witnessed or experienced glossolalia, physical convulsions, and other extreme physical manifestations, which the enthusiasts claimed as signs of the outpouring of the Holy Spirit, perhaps even the outpouring that Joel prophesied for the last days (see Joel 2:28–29). The convulsions were initially related to the miraculous healings, but later they were cultivated for their own sake.

After the cemetery was closed to the public in 1732, the Convulsionaries and their supporters began to meet in private homes, and "the status of the convulsionary became, like that of a medium, half professionalized."[78] Knox reports that there were about eight hundred of them in Paris and the provinces and that their "performances" soon aroused curiosity more than religious or political zeal. The Convulsionaries also invented unusual physical "treatments" to allay the convulsions, which they termed *secours*. These soon became spectacles in themselves, as people were beaten, poked with swords, and even crucified at their own request. Amazingly, many of them reportedly escaped this treatment without harm.[79]

Knox refuses to judge the psychology of this movement, but he stresses that its main ecclesial effect was to divide irreparably the Jansenist movement, from which it had emerged. The existence of the Camisards and the Convulsionaries leads him to conclude that "we ought not to judge the religious temper of the eighteenth century by the religious temper of its political idols or of its literary interpreters.… [T]he age of enlightenment was also an age of fanaticisms."[80]

The Moravian Brethren
In studying "the Moravian tradition," Knox sets the stage for the climax of his book, the analysis of John Wesley and the Methodist

movement. The Moravian tradition had its historical roots in the Utraquists and Taborites of the later Middle Ages and the Church of the Brethren of the Reformation era, but it lost many of its original traits during the hundred years of its dissolution after the Peace of Westphalia. Although the "apostolic succession" within the Brethren church was maintained through Jan Amos Comenius, the religious character of the revived Moravian Brethren owed much more to the spirituality of Philip Spener and German Pietism.[81]

German Pietism's chief center of influence was the University of Halle, where a young German count, Nikolaus von Zinzendorf, was educated early in the eighteenth century. Pietism gave Zinzendorf the idea of forming small groups or "churches" (*ecclesiolae*) of ardent, prayerful believers within the broader church.[82] Zinzendorf's vision was to reunite Christianity by having these vibrant, ecumenical groups leaven the whole Christian church.

When some of the remaining members of the Moravian church came to his estate seeking refuge, Zinzendorf took them in and began to mold them into a prototype of his vision. Although they insisted on retaining their independent ecclesial status, Zinzendorf inserted them as much as possible into his native Lutheran church. He himself was ordained a Lutheran priest and consecrated a Moravian bishop.

Zinzendorf instructed his missionary communities to become participants in the sacramental and prayer life of whatever church was present in their mission field. If there was none, they were to create miniature theocracies by establishing settlements of regimented communal life and strict discipline, "a religious life without celibacy."[83] Because they did not claim to be a church, the Moravians had no uniform body of doctrine but depended for their unity on the continuity of their lifestyle and discipline. They might be termed "ultrasupernaturalists" in that their strict discipline was a protest against the alleged laxity of the churches.[84]

But Moravianism under Zinzendorf was distinctive for more than its discipline. It had a spirituality of its own, which Knox describes as "German Pietism refracted through the curious lens of Zinzendorf's own speculation."[85] The primary theme of that spirituality was Christ as our Redeemer, exemplifying Knox's reference to the chief concern of evangelical enthusiasm: soteriology. During one dark period of Moravianism's history, the "Sifting Time," that spirituality degenerated into a childish sentimentality. At its best it was marked by a quiet joy and peace of mind perceived by the believer as an assurance that he stood in God's favor. It was this assurance of the Moravians that so impressed John Wesley.[86]

Moravianism, like most enthusiastic movements, trusted in the regular intervention of God to guide its affairs. Unlike other such movements, it sought this guidance in large and small matters by drawing lots. "[S]ortilege," Knox comments, "is a natural and logically consistent device of the ultrasupernaturalist."[87] He also remarks that the process of lot-taking was often controlled by the elders of the community, who usually had their way when the community made decisions, regardless of the result of the lot.[88]

Zinzendorf himself chiefly controlled the policy and vision of the *Unitas Fratrum* (another name for Brethren) as long as he lived. He meant it to be "a kind of religious order within the framework of Protestant Christendom, acting as a liaison between the rival sects by confusing its own outline, and remaining always on terms with the religion of the country."[89]

Zinzendorf's ultimate hope was that the Moravian church would disappear after its mission of reconciliation had been achieved. But because he was unable to inculcate this vision into the movement as a whole, Moravianism remained simply another church or denomination within Christianity, as most of the Brethren desired it to be. But it did succeed, Knox adds, in remaining a spiritual elite with a notable spirit of piety and brotherliness among its members.[90]

Methodism

The movement that is the climax of the book, and perhaps the epitome of enthusiasm, is the eighteenth-century Methodist movement led by John Wesley. Knox devotes four chapters of his book, over one-fifth of this six-hundred-page tome, to studying John Wesley and Methodism.

Knox is fascinated with John Wesley and even sympathetic to his cause. This is true, in part, because John Wesley himself shared many of Ronald Knox's concerns and reservations about enthusiasm. In the section of chapter eighteen entitled "Was Wesley an Enthusiast?" Knox argues that *enthusiasm* was synonymous with *fanaticism* in Wesley's time, but he adds that he considers this usage to be inaccurate: "The term 'enthusiast' was used in Wesley's day, and by Wesley himself, with singular want of accuracy. The air would have been cleared if controversialists would have confined themselves to Stinstra's word, 'fanaticism.'"[91]

To substantiate the equivalence of these terms, Knox cites three instances where Wesley uses the term *enthusiast* or *enthusiastic* pejoratively. In one of these Wesley comments on people who seek a revelation of God's will by "visions or dreams, by a strong impression or sudden impulse of the mind": "How frequently do men mistake herein! How they are misled by pride, and a warm imagination, to ascribe such impulses or impressions, dreams, or visions, to God, as are utterly unworthy of him. Now, all this is pure enthusiasm."[92]

Certainly *fanaticism* could be substituted for *enthusiasm* here. Very similar to this is Bishop Gibson's definition of *enthusiasm* from the same period: "a strong persuasion on the mind of persons that they are guided in an extraordinary manner by immediate impressions and impulses of the Spirit of God."[93]

Knox demonstrates successfully that "enthusiasm" is equivalent to "fanaticism" in this period, but he fails to explain why he considers this usage inaccurate. In these chapters on Methodism, he uses the term *enthusiasm* to designate a combination of "inner light" illuminism and any sort of religious emotionalism. He observes that John Wesley "sympathized with enthusiasm…in its most violent forms, yet was never himself carried away by it. The two brothers [John and Charles Wesley], almost alone among the supporters of the movement, kept their heads."[94]

Knox also mentions in two places that John Wesley was ambivalent in his reaction to this enthusiastic tendency: "Wesley the enthusiast, rapt in the communal ecstasy of some consoling love-feast, is being watched all the time by Wesley the experimentalist in religion, who is taking notes, unobtrusively, for his *Journal*."[95]

This phenomenon of Wesley calmly and critically "standing outside of himself," watching himself getting "carried away" in his preaching, is nothing less than "extraordinary" to Knox.[96] Although Wesley's preaching bred enthusiasm, meaning emotionalism and the accompanying physical manifestations, "his pose is one of marble detachment from the passions of his age. He is determined not to be an enthusiast."[97]

It should also be noted that John Wesley, unlike other enthusiasts, believed strongly in the necessity and efficacy of the sacraments of the church, especially the Lord's Supper (the Eucharist). He insisted, for example, that Methodist preaching services not conflict with the Sunday services of the sacramental churches, such as Anglicanism. In fact, Wesley even invited Anglicans who came to hear him preach early Sunday morning to join him in attending the Anglican liturgy afterward.[98]

If enthusiasm is defined in the narrow sense of an exhibition of excessive emotionalism and physical manifestations in connection with religion, then John Wesley cannot be termed an enthusiast. But if we apply to him the other possible descriptions of enthusiasm proposed by Knox, such as expecting "more evident results from the grace of God than we others [expect],"[99] then it is possible to characterize him in this way. He was one of the main contributors to the Evangelical revival that swept through England and the British colonies of America in the eighteenth century.

Other Enthusiastic Movements

The final historical chapter of *Enthusiasm* was intended, Knox says, simply to show that enthusiasm did not disappear upon the death of John Wesley.[100] On the contrary, judging by the impact of Methodism on the English-speaking world, enthusiasm had only begun to have its effect with Wesley. Knox selects three historically distinct movements to illustrate its perdurance: the Irvingites, the Shakers, and the Perfectionists.

The Irvingites are most notable for their revival of the gift of tongues (*glossolalia*), which Knox notes was surprisingly infrequent among enthusiastic movements. He observes:

> All enthusiastic movements are fain to revive, in a more or less degree, the experience of Pentecost; a new outpouring of the Holy Spirit has taken place, and a chosen body of witnesses is there to attest to it. What more likely than that they should aspire to imitate Pentecost in this, its most characteristic manifestation [glossolalia]?[101]

Edward Irving, founder of the movement, manifested this and other enthusiastic traits, such as anti-intellectualism and chiliasm.[102] He and his movement are best remembered for their revival of *glossolalia* and other gifts of the Holy Spirit, which Knox discredits by an unsympathetic account of their nature and exercise. The use of these gifts caused Irving and his followers to be excommunicated from the Presbyterian Church, after which Irving founded the Catholic Apostolic Church. In spite of his historical investigation of this movement, Knox never mentions the much larger twentieth-century movement, Pentecostalism, which Irvingites foreshadowed and which, during Knox's lifetime, was growing in influence.

The Shakers, the "spiritual descendants" of George Fox, are the second movement Knox explores after Wesley. His primary point is to show how the Shakers' fortunes rose and fell with the waves of revivalism that periodically swept over the American continent. "Enthusiasm," he asserts, "does not maintain itself at fever heat"; it is constantly in need of revival.[103]

Finally Knox describes a number of the "perfectionist" sects in nineteenth- and early twentieth-century England and America. Perfectionism is a false conclusion, drawn from the experience of conversion, that it has become impossible for the truly converted believer to sin. The chief difficulty with this doctrine, next to its objective falsity, is the effect it eventually has on the perfectionist's conduct. Knox explains:

> This claim to sinlessness is not to be interpreted in an anti-nomian sense, at least in the first days of a perfectionist movement. It is not that the believer can do what he likes, and everything he does will *ipso facto* be innocent. He has passed into the state in which the angels are; he lives in the Spirit, not in the flesh, and even the enjoyment of the married state has, henceforward, no claim on him and no appeal for him.[104]

The words "in the first days of a perfectionist movement" are important ones here, because Knox employs these movements as examples of groups that attempt to demonstrate their sinlessness, especially in the sexual sphere, or that initially set out to live Christianity without regard to the norms that apply to "ordinary" Christians, and inevitably end up violating basic moral principles.[105] Knox closes this chapter by citing a warning against such excesses proposed by a prominent Quaker, Mrs. Whitall Smith: "Beware of impressions, beware of emotions, beware of physical thrills, beware of voices, beware of everything, in short, that is not according to the strict Bible standard and to your own highest reason."[106]

"Excellent advice," Knox responds. The Bible, he notes, has been cited by every Christian enthusiastic movement to justify its own particular excesses.

For Knox the real issue underlying enthusiasm is whether a man is ultimately guided by "unrestrained private judgment" ("a man's highest reason and his interior impressions") or by "some kind of authority."[107] The enthusiast ultimately chooses "private judgment" of some sort; the traditional, orthodox Christian opts for authority. And for Knox true authority, and not merely a veiled form of private judgment, is only to be found in a visible church that is one, holy, catholic, and apostolic. Knox recognizes this as the Catholic church.

An Evaluation of Knox's Enthusiasm
Ronald Knox's personal experience and temperament cause him to be wary of religious experience, especially as proof of the truth of any doctrine or belief. For him the only reliable basis for belief is the authoritative teaching of Roman Catholicism.

Although Knox never presents a simple definition of enthusiasm, he clearly is referring to an exaggeration or overemphasis of certain Christian beliefs or practices, springing from a desire to live a purer, truer, or more rigorous Christianity than the "average." Knox recognizes that there are many different forms of enthusiasm, the most fundamental division being between the evangelical and mystical varieties. The bulk of his book is devoted to studying movements and groups in Christian history that were in some sense "enthusiastic," examining their particular forms of enthusiasm.

Knox reveals his purpose in writing the book in his preface: "All my historical figures, Wesley himself included, were to be a kind of rogues' gallery, an awful warning against illuminism." And yet, over the course of thirty years of study, his perspective began to change. "[S]omehow, in the writing, my whole treatment of the subject became different; the more you got to know the men, the more human did they become, for better or worse; you were more concerned to find out why they thought as they did than to prove it was wrong."[108] He even begins to sympathize with some enthusiasts, notably John Wesley, the "father" of Methodism.

Knox studies groups that originated in the Catholic church and in the churches of the Reformation, justifying their inclusion in the same book because of one thing they had in common: They broke away from their parent church or institution because they were seeking to live a fuller, purer Christianity. (Ironically, they all ended up becoming "institutionalized" themselves and compromising with "the world" they sought to renounce.) Knox, as a Catholic, ultimately disagrees with this approach (as a Catholic should), even though he sympathizes with some individuals and movements.

But why does Monsignor Knox sympathize with any enthusiast? "Enthusiasm" (according to him) is a false emphasis, an exaggeration, often focusing on things that shouldn't be focused on (for example, religious experience or emotion) and thus leading to distortions of Christian doctrine, practice, or spirituality that either divide or threaten to divide the church. The answer, I think, is that in spite of all his reservations, Ronald Knox realizes that the church does need to be renewed and that, in spite of all their exaggerations and eccentricities, it is the enthusiasts or ultrasupernaturalists who recognize this need and are willing to act on it or at least to express it. In the last two pages of his book, the "climax" of his conclusion, we find his explanation:

> But my aim is to interpret enthusiasm, not to criticize it. If we would interpret it rightly, there is one point that must be seized on above all the rest—in itself enthusiasm is not a wrong tendency but a false emphasis. Quietism exaggerates only a little the doctrine of the mystics about simplicity in prayer, about disinterested love. Quakerism does but enthrone in dangerous isolation the truth of God's presence within us. Jansenism is the vigilant conscience of Christendom overshadowed by a scru-

ple. Methodism is the call back to Christ in an age of Deism. What men like Pascal, Fénelon, and Wesley saw clearly was something true and something valuable; the exaggerations, the eccentricities, were hatched by the heat of controversy. The sympathy which those names evoke is not the index of a rebel spirit in us, who read of them; it is not because they fell foul of authority, and imperiled unity, that we attribute to them greatness. It is not surprising if those who are most sensitive to the needs of their age find their way, sometimes, on to the wrong side of the calendar. Fine instruments are easily spoiled.[109]

Isn't it strange that a book that begins by declaring itself a "trumpet-blast," presenting "a kind of rogues' gallery, an awful warning against illuminism," ends up speaking of the "greatness" of some of the greatest "rogues" in the gallery and seeing the movements that they fostered as basically correct or exaggerating slightly elements of Christianity that are true and important?

The root problem of this book, in my estimation, lies in Monsignor Knox's methodology. He sets out to criticize two things that are distinct but become inseparably intertwined in his description of enthusiasm. The first element of enthusiasm is that it breeds disunity. ("There is, I would say, a recurrent situation in Church history...where an excess of charity threatens unity."[110]) He justifies including a number of disparate historical groups and movements under his umbrella of enthusiasm because they all bred disunity through some criticism of the parent church.

The second element of enthusiasm, for Knox, is that it is based on some religious experience or emotion, which he believes is dangerous and not Catholic. He calls this tendency "ultrasupernaturalism." Catholicism, for him, is based on religious authority, accepted through faith, and not on religious experience or "feeling," not on any direct, immediate perception of God by an individual. Whether the person is a mystical enthusiast, who believes in a direct, personal relationship with God without expecting any particular experience of God, or an evangelical enthusiast, who does expect an assurance, sign, or experience of God's favor and presence, both are basing their Christian lives on something other than faith or the objective signs of the sacraments, creeds, and religious authority.

As one can see, Monsignor Ronald Knox has a rather broad definition of enthusiasm and a correspondingly narrow definition of what it means to be a true ("non-enthusiastic") Catholic or Christian! What is disturbing (at least to a church historian) is that Knox did not develop his description or theory of enthusiasm with sufficient consideration of the numerous individuals, groups, and movements in the history of the Catholic church that have sought to promote church renewal and have been recognized as being truly Catholic. For example, how can one consider the pitfalls of rigorism and illuminism in the early church by looking at Montanism and Donatism, without considering the monastic or ascetic movement?

While entire chapters are spent on the Waldensians, Cathars, and other medieval heresies and schisms, St. Francis of Assisi is mentioned briefly three times, once to claim that he "came too late to immunize society against the anti-clerical germ" and again to say that John Wesley did not admire him and never mentions the mendicant orders in his journal.[111] St. Francis of Assisi's conversion was marked by numerous occasions of God's speaking to him directly, and his prayer often expressed deep emotion and sensitivity to the inner guidance of the Holy Spirit. Why wasn't St. Francis studied by Knox as an enthusiast?

While Knox studies the Anabaptists and George Fox and

Quakerism at length, the saints of the Catholic Reformation are mentioned only in passing. One wonders how Knox can censure as "mystical enthusiasts" those who have experiences of consolation or desolation without considering the lives and teachings of Teresa of Avila and John of the Cross. Knox can draw conclusions about evangelical enthusiasts from the lives of George Whitefield and John Wesley, but what about figures such as Philip Neri and Francis Xavier and the Catholic religious orders whose powerful preaching revitalized the spiritual lives of Catholics, both in Europe and in North America, in the eighteenth and nineteenth centuries? History is replete with saints who had "religious experiences" and were not ashamed to talk about them: St. Paul's encounter on the road to Damascus, St. Augustine's conversion experience, St. Francis of Assisi's words from God received in prayer, St. Teresa of Avila's mystical experiences, St. Philip Neri's "Pentecost," St. John Vianney's battles with demons, not to mention the powerful religious experiences of those Knox does include in his study, including Blaise Pascal and John Wesley.

The weakness of Ronald Knox's *Enthusiasm* lies in his methodology. If he wished to develop an historically cogent theory of enthusiasm, ultrasupernaturalism, or religious experience from a Catholic perspective, he should have included in his study people, groups, and movements with those traits that have been accepted and recognized by the Catholic church as authentically Catholic, as well as ones either condemned by the church or outside the Catholic tradition.

Knox does note that Quietism eventually was accepted by the church but only after the hierarchy condemned its excesses and after its leader, Fénelon, submitted obediently to the church's judgment. Of course, Quietism was no longer an enthusiastic movement after this, according to Knox's first criteria of threatening the church's unity, and as a recognized Catholic spirituality the church no longer considered it ultrasupernaturalistic.

Why does Knox "stack the deck" by limiting his study of enthusiasm to historical examples either marginally Catholic or clearly not Catholic? A simple answer is that he believed that enthusiasm, however well-intentioned, threatened unity and was excessive in its focus on experience. Perhaps it did not occur to him that many of the saints would fit his description of an ultra-supernaturalist. The saints may not have intentionally threatened the church's unity, but their prophetic lives and words challenged the church to reform or renew herself. Could not one who "expects more evident results from the grace of God than we others" be an apt description of a saint and not just "the real character of the enthusiast"?[112]

Ronald Knox was a convert to Catholicism, brought to that faith by an intellectual conversion in a predominantly non-Catholic country. That country was heavily influenced by the Evangelical revival, sparked by John Wesley. It is not surprising that an English Catholic convert turned priest and apologist, who by temperament and culture was suspicious of religious emotion, would desire to write a book chronicling the pitfalls of enthusiastic religion. What *is* perhaps surprising is Knox's discovery, through his research and reflection, of the blessing and even the necessity of enthusiasm. Consider how he ends his book:

> More than all the other Christianities, the Catholic Church is institutional. Her enemies too easily conclude that she is thereby incapacitated from all spiritual initiative, David in Saul's armor; history makes short work of the conclusion. New things as well as old she keeps in her treasure-house; you will

find current coin there, not only obsolete doubloons. But there is danger in her position none the less; where wealth abounds, it is easy to mistake shadow for substance; the fires of spirituality may burn low, and we go on unconscious, dazzled by the glare of tinsel suns. How nearly we thought we could do without St. Francis, without St. Ignatius! Men will not live without vision; that moral we do well to carry away with us from contemplating, in so many strange forms, the record of the visionaries. If we are content with the humdrum, the second-best, the hand-over-hand, it will not be forgiven us. All through the writing of this book I have been haunted by a long-remembered echo of *La Princesse lointaine*:

> *Frére Trophime.* L'inertie est le seul vice, Maître Érasme;
> Et la seule vertu est…
> *Érasme.* Quoi?
> *Frére Trophime.* L'enthousiasme![113]

That is:

> *Brother Trophime.* Inertia is the only vice, sir.
> And the only virtue is…
> *Érasme.* What?
> *Brother Trophime.* Enthusiasm!

Knox's conclusion about enthusiasm appears to boil down to the old saying: "You (the church) can't live with it (because it often leads to various problems and abuses), but you can't live without it (because you'll become stagnant or humdrum)." It also reminds us of the difficulties of an anthropology that neglects or denies the importance of the affective dimension of the human person or a theology that denies that God can approach and "touch" or "speak to" persons affectively and interiorly, and not just through the intellect or the authority of the teaching church.

The limitations of Ronald Knox's methodology and the ambivalence of his conclusion lead me to think that it is more fruitful to identify and evaluate types of renewal that have emerged in the history of Christianity rather than employ his categories of enthusiasm or ultrasupernaturalism. Knox's book serves as a salutary and necessary warning that excesses of various forms and degrees can occur (because they have occurred), sometimes under the guise of being a renewal of the church or of true Christianity, and usually through well-intentioned individuals and groups. As a Catholic, Monsignor Knox sees and appreciates the need for an authority—the authority of the Catholic church's pastors—to discern, correct, and guide expressions of renewal that are susceptible, in their zeal, to excesses, abuse, and division. He is not as concerned about the danger of "quenching" or suppressing the Holy Spirit, because his stated purpose is to warn of the dangers of illuminism or enthusiasm.

From Monsignor Knox's book it is possible to cull some useful guidelines for judging the legitimacy or ecclesiality of renewal groups and movements within the Catholic church.[114] But Knox does not provide advice to help church authorities encourage renewal groups or to enable these groups to use their gifts more effectively to build up the church. The book is primarily cautionary, and thus its main value for those interested in the renewal of the church is to remind them of the danger of this enterprise. In spite of this approach, though, we have seen that even a self-avowed skeptic can come to see, through historical study of even negative examples, the value and the necessity of enthusiastic forms of renewal.

CHAPTER SEVEN

Renewal in the Twentieth and Twenty-first Centuries

Having considered principles of renewal and the history of church renewal from various perspectives, we now come to the most important questions: What is God doing to renew the church now, and how can we members of the church cooperate with the Holy Spirit and contribute to her renewal? How can we, as St. Francis and so many of the saints have done, hear and obey God's call to "rebuild my church"?

To answer these questions, we have to be attentive to the guidance of the Holy Spirit, especially by "reading the signs of the times and interpreting them in the light of the Gospel," as Vatican II's Pastoral Constitution on the Church in the Modern World instructed Catholics to do (*Gaudium et Spes*, 4). In considering how I would undertake this task in this chapter, it occurred to me that a wise and gifted Christian leader already has given us a truly prophetic vision of the renewal of the church as it has entered into the third millennium. This leader is Pope John Paul II, and his pastoral vision for this new era is presented in his Apostolic Letter *Novo Millennio Ineunte,* issued "At the Beginning of the New Millennium," January 6, 2001. It should be noted that many of the pastoral priorities listed in this document have been carried out by Pope Benedict XVI, who closely collaborated with John Paul II for about twenty years as prefect of the Sacred Congregation for the Doctrine of the Faith.

It was noted in a previous chapter that renewal often is brought about "from the top down," by those who serve and lead the church by virtue of their office. Obviously, popes have a particularly strong influence in guiding and renewing the church. In considering this document as a guide for discerning what the Lord has done (in the twentieth century) and possibly will do (in the twenty-first century) to renew the church, we have the benefit of the perspective of the church leader who has done the most to encourage and guide Catholic renewal in the last quarter of the twentieth century and into the century now begun. More than merely an observer of the church's renewal, John Paul II wrote this document in his office as the Catholic church's chief pastor and teacher. Thus the document itself has magisterial authority, which adds to its significance in interpreting what the Holy Spirit is saying to the church in this era.

It is not my purpose to summarize *Novo Millennio Ineunte* but to select themes that have to do with church renewal. The overall theme of the document is characteristic of the pope who told us, "Open wide the doors to Christ!" and, "Do not be afraid!" His message to the church at the beginning of the new millennium is Jesus' admonition to Peter and his companions after a long night of unsuccessful fishing: *Duc in altum,* "Put out into the deep!"

(Luke 5:4), after which "they caught a great number of fish (Lk 5:6)" (*Novo Millennio Ineunte*, 1). This is an encouraging word for those who may be weary in praying and working for renewal, when their efforts appear to be having little result.

John Paul II reminds us that "Christianity is grace" and that our first duty is to praise God for what he has done for us, especially in Christ (*Novo Millennio Ineunte*, 4). This, in fact, was the focus of the Great Jubilee—the two thousandth anniversary of the birth of Jesus, which this apostolic letter commemorates. The first chapter of *Novo Millennio Ineunte* is mainly the pope's reflections on the events of the Jubilee Year and their significance, both in purifying the church from her past sins and refreshing and strengthening her for the future.

The second chapter is devoted to the importance of contemplating the face of Christ our Savior, so we may truly understand who he is and who we are as his followers. The third and fourth chapters—"Starting Afresh from Christ" and "Witnesses to Love"—focus on what the Holy Father believes the Lord wishes to do in the church in the new millennium.

One thing that John Paul insists upon at the beginning of this latter section is that there is no magic formula or new program for going forth into the future: "No, we shall not be saved by a formula but by a Person, and the assurance that he gives us: *I am with you!* It is not therefore a matter of inventing a 'new program.' The program already exists: it is a plan found in the Gospel and the living Tradition, it is the same as ever. Ultimately, it has its center in Christ himself." Pope John Paul insists that "this program for all times is our program for the Third Millennium" (*Novo Millennio Ineunte*, 29).[1]

Now that the Great Jubilee has ended, the church faces "the larger and more demanding challenge of normal pastoral activity" (*Novo Millennio Ineunte*, 29). As we shall see, this does not mean that nothing has changed and the church goes back to "business as usual." The point of this apostolic letter is to present a renewed vision for the future of the church, which comes as a result of the graces and reflections of the Great Jubilee and all that preceded it in preparation.

I will now select some of Pope John Paul's "*pastoral priorities* which the experience of the Great Jubilee has...brought to light" (*Novo Millennio Ineunte*, 29). These priorities represent a powerful prophetic vision of the church's renewal in the twentieth and twenty-first centuries.

In Pope John Paul II's view, renewal
- is guided by the teaching of the Second Vatican Council;
- is ecumenical;
- seeks holiness through prayer and listening and responding to the Word of God;
- lives holiness in every vocation;
- is evangelistic or mission oriented;
- is at the service of others and the world in charity;
- fosters communion or unity within the church and with others;
- involves and even is led by laypeople;
- often comes about through ecclesial movements or groups.

Let us examine each of these characteristics.

Renewal Is Guided by the Teaching of the Second Vatican Council
Ecumenical councils have always been powerful and significant instruments of the Lord for the guidance, reform, and renewal of

his church. They are, in a very real sense, God's word to his church at a particular time in history. And as Vatican II's Dogmatic Constitution on Divine Revelation taught, the only adequate response to God's word is the "obedience of faith" (*Dei Verbum*, 5; Romans 16:26; see Romans 1:5; 2 Corinthians 10:5–6): to hear, believe, and act upon it.

All of the popes since Vatican II have affirmed the centrality of its teaching for the direction and renewal of the church, especially since it was explicitly undertaken as a "council of renewal" for our time. In 1985 Cardinal Joseph Ratzinger affirmed that, despite the challenges to the church after the Second Vatican Council, the solution to those problems was "not to '*turn back*,' but rather, '*to return to the authentic text of the original Vatican II.*'... We must remain faithful to the *today* of the Church, not the *yesterday* or *tomorrow*. And this today of the Church is the documents of Vatican II."[2]

It is notable that even twenty years after the close of the council, Joseph Ratzinger still considered its documents to be the "today" of the church and not the "yesterday." Until another ecumenical council is held, the implementation of this council is the mission of the church.[3] In his first homily as pope, Benedict XVI confirmed Pope John Paul II's statement that "with the passing of the years, *the Council documents have lost nothing of their value or brilliance*" and his allusions to the council as "*the great grace bestowed on the Church in the twentieth century*" and a "sure compass by which to take our bearings in the century now beginning" (*Novo Millennio Ineunte*, 57):

> With the great jubilee the church was introduced into the new millennium carrying in her hands the Gospel, applied to the

world through the authoritative rereading of Vatican Council II. Pope John Paul II justly indicated the council as a "compass" with which to orient ourselves in the vast ocean of the third millennium. Also in his spiritual testament he noted: "I am convinced that for a very long time the new generations will draw upon the riches that this council of the 20th century gave us."

I, too, as I start in the service that is proper to the successor of Peter, wish to affirm with force my decided will to pursue the commitment to enact Vatican Council II, in the wake of my predecessors and in faithful continuity with the millennia-old tradition of the church…. With the passing of time, the conciliar documents have not lost their timeliness; their teachings have shown themselves to be especially pertinent to the new exigencies of the church and the present globalized society.[4]

The Second Vatican Council did not anticipate all that God will do to renew the church in the millennium now begun. Nonetheless, being a council whose main focus was on the nature and mission of the church and on church renewal, I believe that it is correct to say that the renewal of the church will be guided by its teaching.

A question may be raised: "What did Pope Benedict XVI intend when he permitted the liturgy of Trent (the Tridentine Mass) to be celebrated as an 'extraordinary' form?" Does this signal that the revised *ordinary* form of the Mass (the *Novus Ordo*) of Vatican II is somehow insufficient? Judging from his own words, this is not the case. Pope Benedict has allowed the "extraordinary" form of the liturgy to be celebrated primarily as an attempt to reconcile disaffected Catholics (the followers of the late excommunicated

Archbishop Marcel Lefebvre) to the church. It would be a contradiction of Pope Benedict's own words to see the "extraordinary" form Tridentine Mass as an alternative to the *Novus Ordo*, as if any Catholic simply could choose to "opt out" of living according to the norms of Vatican II. They are a true renewal of the church's ancient liturgical roots.

Certainly there have been some difficulties in the implementation of Vatican II in this area, but (to repeat) Pope Benedict's solution to these problems is "not to 'turn back.'... We must remain faithful to the *today* of the Church, not to the *yesterday* or *tomorrow*. And this *today* of the church is the documents of Vatican II."[5] One hopes the "extraordinary" form Tridentine Mass will serve as a bridge to enable disaffected Catholics to return to the *today* of the church—the "ordinary" form of the sacred liturgy that we have by virtue of the Second Vatican Council's Constitution on the Sacred Liturgy (*Sacrosanctum Concilium*).

Renewal Today Is Ecumenical

Pope Leo XIII opened the twentieth century with the invocation of the Holy Spirit, and notable signs of change began soon afterward. One of these was the movement for Christian unity—ecumenism—which began among Protestant and Orthodox communions and eventually was endorsed by the Catholic church. Catholics began to make important new ecumenical initiatives with the Second Vatican Council. Working for the reunification of the church has been a top priority for all the popes since the council. Pope Benedict XVI said in his first homily as pope:

> [I]n full awareness and at the beginning of his ministry in
> the church of Rome that Peter bathed with his blood, the
> current successor assumes as his primary commitment that

of working tirelessly toward the reconstitution of the full and visible unity of all Christ's followers. This is his ambition, this is his compelling duty. He is aware that to do so expressions of good feelings are not enough. Concrete gestures are required to penetrate souls and move consciences, encouraging everyone to that interior conversion which is the basis for all progress on the road of ecumenism.

Theological dialogue is necessary. A profound examination of the historical reasons behind past choices is also indispensable. But even more urgent is that "purification of memory," which was so often evoked by John Paul II, and which alone can dispose souls to welcome the full truth of Christ. It is before him, supreme judge of all living things, that each of us must stand, in the awareness that one day we must explain to him what we did and what we did not do for the great good that is the full and visible unity of all his disciples.

The current successor of Peter feels himself to be personally implicated in this question and is disposed to do all in his power to promote the fundamental cause of ecumenism. In the wake of his predecessors, he is fully determined to cultivate any initiative that may seem appropriate to promote contact and agreement with representatives from the various churches and ecclesial communities. Indeed, on this occasion too, he sends them his most cordial greetings in Christ, the one Lord of all.[6]

The Holy Spirit had begun to renew the Catholic church in the twentieth century in other ways that aided and strengthened her initiative for Christian unity. Vatican II's Decree on Ecumenism states:

> Church renewal…has notable ecumenical importance. Already this renewal is taking place in various spheres of the Church's life; the biblical and liturgical movements, the preaching of the Word of God and catechetics, the apostolate of the laity, new forms of religious life and the spirituality of married life, and the Church's social teaching and activity. All these should be considered as promises and guarantees for the future progress of ecumenism. (*Unitatis Redintegratio*, 6)

The Decree on Ecumenism here mentions just a few of the aspects of renewal that began in the twentieth century. These renewals have ecumenical importance because they are a revitalization of the church in areas where other Christians judged the Catholic church to be either weak or in error. When Catholics began to read and study the Bible more, focus on the role of laypeople in the church (including the spirituality of marriage), celebrate a liturgy in the vernacular that more clearly reflects the liturgy of the early church, with priests preaching homilies based on Scripture and authentic Tradition, other Christians began to take notice. Some even reevaluated their past prejudices about Catholics, especially when Catholics began to make respectful approaches to them as separated brothers and sisters in Christ instead of as heretics or schismatics.

So one characteristic of church renewal today is that God is acting to renew the whole church, across denominational lines and boundaries. The Holy Spirit is renewing the church in similar ways in many Christian communions. This means that Catholics can share perspectives and wisdom concerning renewal with other Christians, as well as learn from other Christians approaches that may help us in our quest for renewal.

The Decree on Ecumenism taught that anything the Holy Spirit does "in the hearts of our separated brethren can contribute to our own edification," because "whatever is truly Christian…can always bring a more perfect realization of the very mystery of Christ and the Church" (*Unitatis Redintegratio*, 4). We also can and should pray with other Christians for the unity and spiritual renewal of the whole Body of Christ (*Unitatis Redintegratio*, 8). Renewal is a common quest of all Christians that can bring us closer together.

Renewal Seeks Holiness Through Prayer and the Word of God
At the heart of every true and significant renewal of the church is the pursuit of holiness. The lives of all the saints who have contributed to the renewal of the church attest to this. Their primary quest was to seek and serve God above all, and the renewal of the church came as a result of that. It is not coincidental that the central chapter (chapter five) of the central document of the Second Vatican Council (*Lumen Gentium*) is devoted to the call of all members of the church to be holy.

No one has understood or expressed the importance of this more than Pope John Paul II. In his list of pastoral priorities for the church in the new millennium, he made this the first priority:

> First of all, I have no hesitation in saying that all pastoral initiatives must be set in relation to *holiness*….
>
> …Once the Jubilee is over, we resume our normal path, but knowing that stressing holiness remains more than ever an urgent pastoral task.
>
> It is necessary therefore to rediscover the full practical significance of Chapter 5 of the Dogmatic Constitution on the Church *Lumen Gentium*, dedicated to the "universal call to

holiness." The Council Fathers laid such stress on this point, not just to embellish ecclesiology with a kind of spiritual veneer, but to make the call to holiness an intrinsic and essential aspect of their teaching on the Church. (*Novo Millennio Ineunte*, 30)

After explaining the meaning of the "gift" of holiness as an essential mark of the church, John Paul proceeded to explain that this gift becomes a task "which must shape the whole of Christian life" (*Novo Millennio Ineunte*, 30). This leads him to ask the important and natural pastoral question, "Can holiness ever be 'planned'? What might the word 'holiness' mean in the context of a pastoral plan?" (*Novo Millennio Ineunte*, 31). If holiness is a key to renewal, he is also raising a key question of this book: "Can renewal ever be planned?" or, "How does a pastoral plan lead to or bring about renewal?"

John Paul's answer implies a plan: All members of the church must be striving tirelessly for holiness and not settle for anything less. (Likewise Catholics should not be satisfied with anything less than a fully renewed church.) He states that one of the consequences of making holiness the goal of all pastoral activity is that Catholics cannot "settle for a life of mediocrity, marked by a minimalistic ethic and a shallow religiosity." When those entering the church are asked if they wish to be baptized, it is the same as asking them, "'Do you wish to become holy?' It means to set before them the radical nature of the Sermon on the Mount: 'Be perfect as your heavenly Father is perfect' (*Mt* 5:48)" (*Novo Millennio Ineunte*, 31).

Perhaps then the fundamental, "root" reason we'll find whenever or wherever the church is not being renewed is complacency: Catholics are comfortable and satisfied with far too little. The solution? The pope thought it was to call God's people on to holiness, and he explains how this is possible for everyone:

> As the Council itself explained, this ideal of perfection must not be misunderstood as if it involved some kind of extraordinary existence, possible only for a few "uncommon heroes" of holiness.... The time has come to re-propose wholeheartedly to everyone this *high standard of ordinary Christian living*: the whole life of the Christian community and of Christian families must lead in this direction. It is also clear however that the paths to holiness are personal and call for a genuine "*training in holiness*," adapted to people's needs. (*Novo Millennio Ineunte*, 31)

John Paul II was a realist. The church will not be fully renewed, or even make significant progress toward this, unless the parish community (the basic Christian community) and Catholic families are striving for holiness and providing some practical training that their members receive and enter into with openness and desire.

The first and most essential aspect of this "training in holiness," which is also the first step toward renewal of the church, is learning to pray—and then to pray! As Pope John Paul II explained: "This training in holiness calls for a Christian life distinguished above all *in the art of prayer*," both "in the liturgy, the summit and source of the Church's life [see *Sacrosanctum Concilium*, 10]," and also "in personal [prayer] experience." This, he said, "is the secret of a truly vital Christianity" (*Novo Millennio Ineunte*, 32).

John Paul recommended a study of the "great mystical tradition of the Church of both East and West.... It shows how prayer can progress, as a genuine dialogue of love, to the point of rendering the person wholly possessed by the divine Beloved, vibrating at the Spirit's touch, resting filially within the Father's heart" (*Novo Millennio Ineunte*, 33). He mentions specifically the "teachings of St. John of the Cross and St. Teresa of Avila" among the "many shining examples" of this mystical tradition of prayer. His conclusion:

> Yes, dear brothers and sisters, our Christian communities must become *genuine "schools" of prayer*, where the meeting with Christ is expressed not just in imploring help but also in thanksgiving, praise, adoration, contemplation, listening and ardent devotion, until the heart truly "falls in love." Intense prayer, yes, but it does not distract us from our commitment to history: by opening our heart to the love of God it also opens it to the love of our brothers and sisters, and makes us capable of shaping history according to God's plan....
>
> It is therefore essential that *education in prayer* should become in some way a key-point of all pastoral planning. (*Novo Millennio Ineunte*, 33, 34)

Two points may be noted here. First, the church should affirm and promote the art of prayer—in thanksgiving, praise, adoration, contemplation, listening, and ardent devotion—wherever it is being taught and practiced. Secondly, intense prayer is not to be seen as something opposed to service of others and the world. In fact, prayer is the source of power and strength both for the renewal of the church and for the mission of the church in the world, including evangelization, social justice, and charitable works.

Accompanying prayer in the pursuit of holiness is the prayerful reading and study of Sacred Scripture. Pope John Paul noted:

There is no doubt that this primacy of holiness and prayer is inconceivable without a renewed *listening to the word of God.* Ever since the Second Vatican Council underlined the pre-eminent role of the word of God in the life of the Church, great progress has certainly been made in devout listening to Sacred Scripture and attentive study of it.... [T]his development needs to be consolidated and deepened, also by making sure that every family has a Bible. It is especially necessary that listening to the word of God should become a life-giving encounter, in the ancient and ever valid tradition of *lectio divina*, which draws from the biblical text the living word which questions, directs and shapes our lives. (*Novo Millennio Ineunte*, 39)

A Note on the Challenge of Liturgical Renewal

The liturgy, as the formal gathering of God's faithful people to pray and worship the Lord, is intended to be a primary source and expression of the church's power and unity. Sadly, because of misunderstandings of Vatican II and other church teachings, sometimes the liturgy has become a "lightning rod" exposing tension and even division in the church. This must be corrected if the liturgy is truly to be an expression of unity and a source of power for the life and renewal of the church. This is certainly an important priority and task for the church in many places at the beginning of the third millennium.

The 1985 Extraordinary Synod of Bishops, in evaluating the implementation of Vatican II with regard to the liturgy, stated: "The liturgical renewal is the most visible fruit of the whole conciliar effort. Even if there have been some difficulties, it has generally been received joyfully and fruitfully by the faithful."[7]

However, many Catholics today criticize the use of the vernacular and contemporary musical instruments and hymns as a false renewal that is actually a concession (or a surrender) to the decadent, secular culture of the modern world. They blame the changes in the liturgy for steeply declining Mass attendance in the West and for a loss of the "sense of the sacred," which (they say) Latin, the pipe organ, and Gregorian chant preserve. To them the liturgical renewal of Vatican II is a failure and even a scandal.

In discerning what is authentic renewal, I think we need to undertake an analysis that goes beyond externals or appearances. With regard to the liturgy, the Second Vatican Council promoted as its primary goal the "full, conscious, and active participation in liturgical celebrations which is demanded by the very nature of the liturgy" (*Sacrosanctum Concilium*, 14). The liturgy is "an action of Christ the Priest and of his Body, which is the Church" (*Sacrosanctum Concilium*, 7); the faithful are not spectators but active participants. Vatican II sought, among other things, to promote the active or (more properly translated) *real* participation of all the faithful in the liturgy.

Language and music are two means of enabling the congregation to enter into the mystery of Christ's presence and the worship of God more fully. As the Extraordinary Synod stated:

> The active participation so happily increased after the Council does not consist only in external activity, but above all in interior and spiritual participation, in living and fruitful participation in the paschal mystery of Jesus Christ (cf. *Sacrosanctum Concilium*, no. 11). It is evident that the liturgy must favor the sense of the sacred and make it shine forth. It must be permeated by the spirit of reverence, adoration and the glory of God.[8]

Some Catholics may be led into this "interior and spiritual partic-ipation" more effectively by a Latin Mass with Gregorian chant and pipe organ accompaniment, others by a vernacular Mass with guitars or keyboard accompanying contemporary music. Catholicism has always honored the principle of catholic diver-sity, with unity in essentials. One would hope that either type of Mass celebrated with "the spirit of reverence, adoration and the glory of God" would be appreciated by any Catholic or at least be recognized as an authentically Catholic liturgy. Certainly if the church is to be fully renewed, Catholics must overcome wran-gling and division over this issue; all magisterially approved forms of liturgical worship ought to be accepted, with room for the Holy Spirit to act and to guide the church, enabling us to wor-ship "in spirit and truth" (John 4:24).

Renewal Is Evangelistic or Mission Oriented

The Second Vatican Council taught that "[t]he Church on earth is by its very nature missionary" (*Ad Gentes Divinitus*, 2). In the years following the Council, some confusion arose concerning the necessity of the church's missionary mandate. In 1976 Pope Paul VI issued a powerful encyclical letter, "On Evangelization in the Modern World" (*Evangelii Nuntiandi*), and in 1990 Pope John Paul II wrote "Mission of the Redeemer" (*Redemptoris Missio*). Both of these underscored Jesus' mandate to "make disciples of all nations" (Matthew 28:19), heeding St. Paul's words, "Woe to me if I do not preach the gospel!" (1 Corinthians 9:16). These popes called for a renewed fervor of the entire church in the proclama-tion of the gospel of Christ, both in word and action.

This evangelization is to be directed not only to those who have not yet heard of Jesus Christ ("missionary activity," properly speaking) but also to those who either have fallen away from their Christian heritage or cling to a diluted or distorted form of Christianity. Pope John Paul II referred to this reawakened, renewed missionary fervor as the "new evangelization." In his 2001 letter he urged:

> [T]his is surely a priority for the Church at the dawn of the new millennium. Even in countries evangelized many centuries ago, the reality of a "Christian society"...is now gone. Today we must courageously face a situation which is becoming increasingly diversified and demanding, in the context of "globalization" and of the consequent new and uncertain mingling of peoples and cultures. Over the years I have often repeated the summons to the *new evangelization....* [W]e must ...allow ourselves to be filled with the ardor of the apostolic preaching which followed Pentecost....
>
> ...This passion will not fail to stir in the Church a new sense of mission, which cannot be left to a group of "specialists" but must involve...all the members of the People of God. Those who have come into genuine contact with Christ cannot keep him for themselves, they must proclaim him. A new apostolic outreach is needed, which will be lived as *the everyday commitment of Christian communities and groups....*
>
> Christ must be presented to all people with confidence. (*Novo Millennio Ineunte*, 40)

A renewed church will express this renewal through vibrant witness to Jesus Christ. Likewise, no church or community within the church can claim to be fully renewed unless it is, in some way, evangelistic (proclaiming Christ in word and deed) in its outlook and its activity.

Renewal Is at the Service of Others and of the World

Earlier we noted that prayer does not distract the Christian from charity or taking responsibility for the world. Vatican II's Pastoral Constitution on the Church in the Modern World stressed the obligation of Christians to seek after justice and to fulfill their social obligations as an expression of their faith (see *Gaudium et Spes*, 30, 34, 43). "[W]e must reject the temptation to offer a privatized and individualistic spirituality which ill accords with the demands of charity" (*Novo Millennio Ineunte*, 52).

Charity must be the most important distinguishing mark of the life of the church. Pope John Paul notes that "charity of its nature opens out into a service that is universal" and challenges the church in the new millennium to see how far it can go in showing charity to the poorest (*Novo Millennio Ineunte*, 49).

> If we have truly started out anew from the contemplation of Christ, we must learn to see him especially in the faces of those with whom he himself wished to be identified: "I was hungry and you gave me food..." (*Mt* 25:35–37). By these words, no less than by the orthodoxy of her doctrine, the Church measures her fidelity as the Bride of Christ.
>
> Certainly we need to remember that no one can be excluded from our love.... Yet...there is a special presence of Christ in the poor, and this requires the Church to make a preferential option for them. (*Novo Millennio Ineunte*, 49)

As Pope Benedict XVI taught in his third encyclical letter, *Charity in Truth*, issued on June 29, 2009: "Charity is at the heart of the church's social doctrine. Every responsibility and every commitment [spelled] out by that doctrine derives from charity" (*Caritas in Veritate*, 2). The effective renewal of the church is ultimately measured by charity, which Pope Benedict calls the "synthesis of the entire law (see Mt 22:36–40)." Any renewal that does not result in greater love of God and love of neighbor is of questionable value—though this charity and service may be manifest in many ways and is not always visible or measurable by the outside observer.

St. Paul said, "If I give away all I have, and if I deliver my body to be burned, but have not love, I gain nothing" (1 Corinthians 13:3). Only God sees the heart. Growing in service of others in genuine love is an essential task and sign of the church's renewal.

Renewal Fosters Communion, Unity
The Letter to the Ephesians exhorts Christians:

> Walk in a manner worthy of the calling to which you have been called, with all lowliness, and meekness, with patience, forbearing one another in love, eager to maintain the unity of the Spirit in the bond of peace. There is one body and one Spirit, just as you were called to the one hope that belongs to your call, one Lord, one faith, one baptism, one God and Father of us all, who is above all and through all and in all….
>
> …Speaking the truth in love, we are to grow up in every way into him who is the head, into Christ, from whom the whole body, joined and knit together by every joint with which it is supplied, when each part is working properly, makes bodily growth and upbuilds itself in love. (Ephesians 4:1–6, 15–16)

"The church is one" is the first "mark" or characteristic of the church. The Extraordinary Synod of 1985 stressed that communion is the "central and fundamental idea of the Council's document." What is communion?

> Fundamentally it is a matter of communion with God through
> Jesus Christ in the Holy Spirit. This communion is had in the
> Word of God and in the sacraments. Baptism is the door and
> the foundation of communion in the Church. The Eucharist is
> the source and the culmination of the whole Christian life (cf.
> *Lumen Gentium*, no. 11). The communion of the Eucharistic
> Body of Christ signifies and produces, that is, builds up the
> intimate communion of all the faithful in the Body of Christ
> which is the Church (1 Cor 10:16).[9]

Pope John Paul II observed that true communion cannot exist
without a "spirituality of communion," which, through contemplating the blessed Trinity, comes to see all others in light of the
unity all humans share in God. It especially will value those who
belong to the church and the gifts they possess. Practically, this
spirituality leads to "the ability to see what is positive in others,
to welcome and prize it as a gift from God: not only as a gift for
the brother or sister…but also as a 'gift for me'…to know how
to 'make room' for our brothers and sisters, bearing 'each other's
burdens' (*Gal* 6:2) and resisting the selfish temptations which…
provoke competition, careerism, distrust and jealousy" (*Novo
Millennio Ineunte*, 43).

We have seen in the historical study in this book that there is
no authentic renewal that divides the church that does not ultimately foster unity within the church. However, there is a danger
that true movements of renewal can appear to be divisive because
they sometimes challenge and confront error, complacency, and
lukewarmness. Renewal movements and figures are prophetic:
They present a word from God for the church. They are not
always popular, even among those who are in some way "their
own." Jesus said, "A prophet is not without honor, except in his

own country, and among his own kin, and in his own house" (Mark 6:4).

Throughout the church's history, authentic renewal movements and individuals seeking the renewal of the church have met with opposition or reservations, even from church authorities, simply because they were advocating something new, that is, something different from the status quo. Pope Benedict XVI, before his pontificate, observed that local churches may fall into a "conformist *modus vivendi* with the world;...the salt can lose its flavor." He alluded to Kierkegaard's acute criticism of the established Church of Denmark in the nineteenth century and noted, "Even if the departure from the radical demands of the Gospel has not reached the point that provoked Kierkegaard's denunciation, the irruption of the new is nonetheless experienced as a disruption."[10] He dismissed the "blasé attitude of intellectual superiority that immediately brands the zeal of those seized by the Holy Spirit and their uninhibited faith with the anathema of fundamentalism, and only authorizes a faith in which the ifs and buts are more important than the substance of what is believed."[11]

Renewal is "disruptive" in that it upsets the status quo and calls for a more vibrant adherence to the gospel or some important aspect of it. So Christians, and especially church authorities, run the risk of stifling or quenching the Holy Spirit if they are not open to his action, which after all is a gift of God to the church. Pope John Paul II, in the context of his "spirituality of communion," suggested one approach to prevent this possibility of stifling the Spirit:

> To this end, we need to make our own the ancient pastoral wisdom which, without prejudice to their authority, encouraged Pastors to listen more widely to the entire People of God.

Significant is St. Benedict's reminder to the Abbot of a monastery, inviting him to consult even the youngest members of the community: "By the Lord's inspiration, it is often a younger person who knows what is best." And St. Paulinus of Nola urges: "Let us listen to what all the faithful say, because in every one of them the Spirit of God breathes." (*Novo Millennio Ineunte*, 45)

This is wise advice. If church authorities ignore the insights and aspirations of those who strive for the church's renewal, those people may become frustrated, discouraged, or alienated, and they even may leave the church. If church authorities treat renewal groups and movements like sects (labeling them "fundamentalist," "overzealous," and the like), that is what they might become. Individuals, groups, and movements that seek renewal and desire to be in the heart of the church should be welcomed and shown how they can serve and enrich the parish, diocese, and broader church with their particular gifts and graces.

Both Pope Benedict and Pope John Paul indicated that church leaders should be open to (rather than threatened by) renewal and should show respect for those promoting it. They need a certain "holy fear" before the Lord, who may well be seeking to renew his church through these people. The discernment of how the renewal can benefit the church might take the form of a dialogue: "This is how it seems to me that you can serve the church/parish/diocese. How does that sound to you? Does it fit with your call and charism? Is there any other way you think you could contribute, or your gift could benefit the church?"

Likewise, those promoting renewal should be asking their pastors how they can serve and support the pastors' needs and priorities. The goal of this dialogue is a growth of true communion and the building up or renewal of the church.

We should not be under any illusion that the achievement of communion and the successful renewal of the church will be easy. (After all, we are also opposing Satan and the spiritual enemies of the church and her true renewal.) As Pope Benedict taught:

> Above all, a concept of *communio*, in which the highest pastoral value is attached to the avoidance of conflict, should be rejected. Faith remains a sword and may demand conflict for the sake of truth and love (cf. *Mt* 10:34). A concept of Church unity in which conflicts are dismissed *a priori* as polarization, and in which internal peace is bought at the price of the renunciation of the totality of witness, would quickly prove to be illusory.[12]

The lives of many of the great saints who brought about the renewal and strengthening of the church confirm this truth. Faithful witnesses to God's work will meet opposition, but in the end we pray and trust that God's will, finally, will be accomplished. Ultimately, true renewal will foster a deeper unity and communion in the church, which will be a sure and reliable sign of a genuine action of the Holy Spirit.[13]

Open to the Gifts of the Holy Spirit
This characteristic of renewal—its charismatic dimension—is closely linked to its producing unity or communion, its involving laypeople, and its growth and spread through ecclesial movements. The charismatic dimension could be presented as a feature of these three aspects of renewal, but it merits a separate discussion because it is a dimension of the church and its renewal that is often misunderstood.

The charisms are listed (at least partially, since no list is presented as comprehensive) in the Pauline literature: 1 Corinthians 12–14; Romans 12:3–8; and Ephesians 4:7–16. The charisms are related to the church's unity or communion in that their primary purpose is "for building up the body of Christ, until we all attain to the unity of the faith and of the knowledge of the Son of God" (Ephesians 4:12, 13; see 1 Corinthians 12:7; Romans 12:4–6). The charisms are central to St. Paul's understanding of the church as the "body of Christ," which is a mystery of unity yet in a diversity that is necessary for the church's completion, proper function, and fulfillment of the mission Jesus has entrusted to it.

After describing the importance of the church's unity and a "spirituality of communion" in the new millennium, John Paul II explained:

> Such a vision of community is closely linked to the Christian community's ability to make room for all the gifts of the Spirit. The unity of the Church is not uniformity, but an organic blending of legitimate diversities. It is the reality of many members joined in a single body, the one Body of Christ (cf. 1 Cor 12:12) (*Novo Millennio Ineunte*, 46).

St. Paul's understanding is that all of the gifts of the Holy Spirit, working together, build communion and strengthen the unity of the church, not divide it. These gifts of the Spirit are given freely to all Christians (see 1 Corinthians 12:7), including laypeople. According to the Second Vatican Council's Decree on the Apostolate of the Laity, the charisms (citing 1 Corinthians 12) are the necessary "equipment" that God provides the laity to carry out their mission or apostolate. "From the reception of these charisms, even the most ordinary ones, there arises for each of the faithful the right and duty of exercising them in the Church and in the world for the good of men and the development of the Church, of exercising them in the freedom of the Holy Spirit who 'breathes where he wills' (Jn 3:8)" (*Apostolicam Actuositatem*, 3).

This aspect of the renewal of the church awaits realization in the Catholic church. Most Catholics still do not recognize or understand the charisms listed by St. Paul, much less their importance for building up the church and their necessity for the church's apostolate. And often Catholics are not permitted to exercise these gifts in "the freedom of the Holy Spirit who 'breathes where he wills.'" (Sadly, perhaps that is a contributing factor for those Catholics who receive these gifts and then leave for Pentecostal church bodies.) The rediscovery by the whole church (and not just by a group or movement within it) of the church's charismatic dimension and the regular use of these charisms are essential for renewal. The recent popes have recognized the "co-essentiality" of this aspect of the church, with the sacraments and the hierarchy.

There is hope that this renewal has begun through new ecclesial movements and groups. When Pope John Paul II invited these movements and communities to Rome in 1998, the year that he devoted to the Holy Spirit in preparation for the Great Jubilee, he addressed this assembly of half a million people with these words:

> Whenever the Spirit intervenes, he leaves people astonished. He brings about events of amazing newness; he radically changes persons and history. This was the unforgettable experience of the Second Vatican Ecumenical Council during which, under the guidance of the same Spirit, the Church rediscovered the charismatic dimension as one of her

constitutive elements. [Here Pope John Paul quotes *Lumen Gentium*, 12.]

The institutional and charismatic aspects are co-essential... to the Church's constitution. They contribute, although differently, to the life, renewal and sanctification of God's People. It is from this providential rediscovery of the Church's charismatic dimension that, before and after the Council, a remarkable pattern of growth has been established for ecclesial movements and new communities....

Today, I would like to cry out to all of you gathered here in St. Peter's Square and to all Christians: Open yourselves docilely to the gifts of the Spirit! Accept gratefully and obediently the charisms which the Spirit never ceases to bestow on us! Do not forget that every charism is given for the common good, that is, for the benefit of the whole Church.[14]

Renewal is, above all, a work of the Holy Spirit. Is it surprising that the renewal of the church in this era is marked by an abundant outpouring of the gifts with which the Holy Spirit equips the church for her growth and mission? As we have seen, these gifts are an important aspect of the renewal of the laity's role in the mission of the church and of the emergence of new ecclesial movements and communities that have been part of the church's renewal in our time.

Renewal Is Marked by Increased Lay Involvement and Leadership
The full renewal of the church always involves all of her members —the ordained (clergy), religious, and the lay faithful—but at this time in history it is the laity whose role is distinctive. Why?

Prior to the Second Vatican Council, many laypeople saw themselves primarily as recipients of the church's ministry and teaching instead of active agents carrying out the mission of the church. They realized that they needed to contribute regularly to the Sunday collection, support Catholic schools and institutions, and pray for the needs of the church. The teaching of the council revolutionized their understanding as sharers in the threefold ministry of Jesus as priest, prophet, and king (see *Lumen Gentium*, 21).

What Vatican II presented was a renewed vision of a vibrant united church, with all its members working together to proclaim Christ and advance the reign of God in this world. *Sacrosanctum Concilium* makes it clear that "public worship is performed by the Mystical Body of Jesus Christ, that is, by the Head and his members…. [E]very liturgical celebration…is an action of Christ the Priest and of his Body, which is the Church" (*Sacrosanctum Concilium*, 7). Laity, therefore, "by virtue of their royal priesthood, participate in the offering of the Eucharist" (*Lumen Gentium*, 10).

Furthermore, "[Christ] fulfills this prophetic office, not only by the hierarchy…but also by the laity," who are witnesses to Christ and his kingdom in daily life by their words and deeds. "The laity can, and must, do valuable work for the evangelization of the world" (*Lumen Gentium*, 35).

Finally, regarding the kingly office of Christ, Vatican II says, "The Lord also desires that his kingdom be spread by the lay faithful…. [B]y their secular activity they help one another achieve greater holiness of life, so that the world may be filled with the spirit of Christ and may the more effectively attain its destiny in justice, in love and in peace" (*Lumen Gentium*, 36).

Vatican II's Decree on the Apostolate of the Laity insists that there are to be no passive or inactive laypeople in the church:

> The Church was founded to spread the kingdom of Christ over all the earth for the glory of God the Father, to make all

men partakers in redemption and salvation, and through them to establish the right relationship of the entire world to Christ. Every activity of the Mystical Body with this in view goes by the name of "apostolate."...

[T[he Christian vocation is, of its nature, a vocation to the apostolate as well.... [A] member [of the Body of Christ] who does not work at the growth of the body to the extent of his possibilities must be considered useless both to the Church and to himself.

...The characteristic of the lay state being a life led in the midst of the world and of secular affairs, laymen are called by God to make of their apostolate, through the vigor of their Christian spirit, a leaven in the world. (*Apostolicam Actuositatem*, 2)

These themes were echoed and further developed at the Synod of Bishops on the Laity called by Pope John Paul II in 1987. The pope's apostolic exhortation On the Lay Members of Christ's Faithful People (December 30, 1988) includes some of the topics discussed in this chapter, such as the importance of the charisms of the laity for building up the church (*Christifideles Laici*, 24) and the emergence of a plethora of lay groups and movements in the church, so much so that Pope John Paul said, "We can speak of *a new era of group endeavors* of the lay faithful" (*Christifideles Laici*, 29).

Whether as individuals or in groups, laypeople are increasingly involved in the renewal of the church at this time in history. (The reader may be able to provide some—perhaps even numerous—examples.) There is sometimes resistance to this involvement, and it has been necessary to clarify the proper roles of laypeople. In general, however, the growth in lay involvement and leadership in the renewal of the church is a positive and healthy sign, a sign that the call of Vatican II for a more active involvement of the laity in the church's life is being heeded.

Pope Benedict XVI has boldly stated:

> [I]t is necessary to improve pastoral structures in such a way that the co-responsibility of all the members of the People of God in their entirety is gradually promoted, with respect for vocations and for the respective roles of the consecrated and of lay people.
>
> This demands a change in mindset, particularly concerning lay people. They must no longer be viewed as "collaborators" of the clergy but truly recognized as "co-responsible" for the Church's being and action, thereby fostering the consolidation of a mature and committed laity.[15]

This would certainly apply to efforts for the renewal of the church. Some significant renewal movements have been founded or led by laypeople.

Renewal Is Brought About by Ecclesial Movements and Communities
In the section of *Novo Millennio Ineunte* on "The Primacy of Grace," Pope John Paul II wrote:

> There is a temptation which perennially besets every spiritual journey and pastoral work: that of thinking that the results depend on our ability to act and to plan. God of course asks us really to cooperate with his grace, and therefore invites us to invest all our resources of intelligence and energy in serving the cause of the Kingdom. But it is fatal to forget that "without Christ we can do nothing" (cf. *Jn* 15:5). (*Novo Millennio Ineunte*, 38)

Church renewal is above all a grace. And nothing demonstrates this truth as clearly as the emergence of groups and movements that have helped renew the church throughout her history. Though perhaps Catholics should expect them by now, they always appear as "surprises of the Holy Spirit." As then Cardinal Joseph Ratzinger observed in 1985:

> What is hopeful at the level of the universal Church…is the rise of new movements which nobody had planned and which nobody has called into being, but which have sprung spontaneously from the inner vitality of the faith itself. What is manifested in them…is something like a pentecostal season in the Church. I am thinking, say, of the charismatic movement, of the Cursillos, of the movement of the Focolare, of the neo-catechumenal communities, of Communion and Liberation….
>
> What is striking is that all this fervor was not elaborated by any office of pastoral planning, but somehow sprang forth by itself….
>
> What is emerging here is a new generation of the Church which I am watching with a great hope. I find it marvelous that the Spirit is once more stronger than our programs and brings himself into play in an altogether different way than we had imagined. In this sense the renewal [of the Church] is afoot.[16]

The pope also commented on the fervor, the "joy of the faith," and the "intense life of prayer" in these groups.

Thirteen years later Cardinal Ratzinger confirmed this evaluation in his opening address to the World Congress of the Ecclesial Movements sponsored by the Pontifical Council of the Laity, held on the days immediately preceding the historic gathering of members of these ecclesial movements with Pope John Paul II on Pentecost 1998. In his address the cardinal said that "the apostolic movements appear in ever new forms in history— necessarily so, because they are the Holy Spirit's answer to the ever changing situations in which the Church lives." He also repeated that movements cannot be produced, established, or systematically promoted by ecclesiastical authority, because they are gifts of God. We should be grateful "that, through all her trials and tribulations, the Church has always succeeded in finding room for all the great new awakenings of the spirit that emerge in her midst."[17]

Who are these ecclesial groups and movements? It is beyond the scope of this book to identify them and discuss their individual characteristics and histories. Some of them preceded the Second Vatican Council, such as the Christian Family Movement. Some movements, such as Focolare, Cursillo, the Emmanuel Community, and Student Youth (the initial form of Communion and Liberation), began before the Second Vatican Council but experienced rapid growth during and especially after the council. Most of them had human founders: Pierre Goursat (Emmanuel), Chiara Lubich (Focolare), Jean Vanier (L'Arche), Monsignor Luigi Giussani (Communion and Liberation), Kiko Arguello (Neocatechumenal Way), and so on. One movement, the charismatic renewal (or "renewal in the Spirit"), was the result of a sovereign outpouring of the Holy Spirit in many parts of the world and thus claims no human founder.

There is no doubt that the teaching of the Second Vatican Council, especially its teachings on renewal, the charisms, and the role of the laity, sparked and encouraged the formation and rapid growth of many of these ecclesial groups and movements.

The Holy Spirit was opening the way for them through the council and continues to do so.

Discerning and Pastoring Ecclesial Movements and Groups
With such an abundance and diversity of renewal groups and movements appearing in the twentieth and twenty-first centuries, one challenge has been to discern which are authentic instruments of renewal and to guide or pastor them so that they are successfully integrated into the church's life. The Catholic church has centuries of experience and wisdom to draw upon in undertaking this task. Movements and groups have brought about or contributed to the renewal of different dimensions of the church's life: prayer, liturgy, sacraments, morality, Scripture, charisms, priestly ministry, religious life, and so on. Some movements and groups have been accorded a distinctive, recognized (even "canonical") form and identity within the church: religious communities and orders, secular institutes, pious unions, third orders, associations of the faithful, and so on. The Catholic church appreciates this diversity, as it reflects the beneficence and creativity of God, who gives the grace that produces all these forms of renewal and of Christian life.

Two recent popes, John Paul II and Benedict XVI, have exhibited extraordinary ability and insight in discerning and guiding the ecclesial groups and movements that have been so evident during their pontificates. (The same could be said of Pope Paul VI and other popes of the twentieth century.) Other church leaders can certainly learn from their teaching and example.

POPE JOHN PAUL II'S CRITERIA
Pope John Paul II, in his 1988 letter The Lay Members of Christ's Faithful People, presented some guidelines for discerning and

guiding predominantly lay groups and movements. He affirmed "first of all, the *freedom for lay people in the Church to form such groups*" (*Christifideles Laici*, 29). He also listed "*clear and definite criteria for discerning and recognizing* such lay groups, also called 'Criteria of Ecclesiality'" (*Christifideles Laici*, 30). These include

- the primacy given to the call of every Christian to holiness
- the responsibility of professing the Catholic faith
- the witness to a strong and authentic communion in filial relationship to the pope and with the local bishop
- conformity to and participation in the Church's apostolic goals (see *Apostolicam Actuositatem*, 20), with "a missionary zeal"
- commitment to a presence in human society, which, in light of the Church's social doctrine, places it at the service of the total dignity of the person (*Christifideles Laici*, 30)

These measures of ecclesiality, as we have mentioned, have been drawn from the church's long experience of discerning groups and movements throughout her history. Besides these more theoretical measures, *Christifideles Laici* notes that the validity of these groups and movements can be seen

> in the *actual fruits* that various group forms show in their organizational life and the works they perform, such as: the renewed appreciation for prayer, contemplation, liturgical and sacramental life, the reawakening of vocations to Christian marriage, the ministerial priesthood and the consecrated life; a readiness to participate in programs and Church activities at the local, national and international levels; a commitment to catechesis and a capacity for teaching and forming Christians; a desire to be present as Christians in various settings of social life and the creation and awakening of charitable, cultural and

spiritual works; the spirit of detachment and evangelical poverty leading to a greater generosity in charity towards all; conversion to the Christian life or the return to Church communion of those baptized members who have fallen away from the faith. (*Christifideles Laici*, 30)

Jesus said that we would know a good tree from a bad one by its fruits (see Matthew 7:20); renewal groups and movements (including the lay groups and movements being discussed) will ultimately be judged by the fruit they bear. "By this my Father is glorified, that you bear much fruit, and so prove to be my disciples" (John 15:8).

Pope John Paul's approach to renewal groups and movements was marked primarily by affirmation and encouragement. However, he was not blind to their shortcomings. In his 1998 Pentecost address to ecclesial movements and groups, he challenged them to enter into a new stage of their life and contribution to the church, "that of ecclesial maturity." He explained that in the birth and spread of these movements, their "unexpected newness which is sometimes even disruptive" gave rise to "questions, uneasiness and tensions" in the church. He characterized this as "a testing period for their fidelity" and "an important occasion for verifying the authenticity of their charisms." However, "today a new stage is unfolding before you: that of ecclesial maturity. This does not mean that all problems have been solved. Rather, it is a challenge. A road to take. The Church expects from you the 'mature' fruits of communion and commitment."[18]

"Ecclesial maturity" has thus become an important theme of reflection and discussion within renewal movements.

THE GUIDANCE OF POPE BENEDICT XVI

Only a couple days before this Pentecost address, Cardinal Ratzinger presented his keynote talk to the World Congress of the Ecclesial Movements in Rome, titled "The Ecclesial Movements: A Theological Reflection on Their Place in the Church." He presented important perspectives and guidelines for ecclesial groups and movements that show his extraordinary wisdom and insight on the topic. He observed that some of the disruption in the church caused by these movements was natural: "Every irruption of the Holy Spirit always upsets human plans." However, he also noted:

> [T]hese movements had their share of childhood diseases. The power of the Spirit could be felt in them, but the Spirit works through human beings and does not simply free them from their weaknesses. There were tendencies to exclusivity and one-sidedness, and hence the inability to involve themselves in the life of the local Church. Buoyed up by their youthful élan, they were convinced that the local Church had, as it were, to crank itself up to their level, to adapt itself to their form, and not vice versa.[19]

The movements, he explained, did not want to be "dragged" into a structure that they felt would repress their life and charism. As a result, "Frictions arose, in which both sides were at fault in different ways." This, Cardinal Ratzinger observed, is the perennial issue of how "the spiritual revival" can relate rightly to "the permanent structure of the Church's life, i.e. the parish and the diocese." This issue will not go away, because "there are ever new irruptions of the Holy Spirit, which continually revitalize and renew that structure. But this renewal hardly ever occurs entirely without pain and friction."[20]

Renewing the Parish: A Pastoral Challenge

Perhaps the greatest challenge of church renewal is bringing the full vision and reality of a renewed church into the normal, everyday life of the parish, what Pope John Paul referred to as "the larger and more demanding challenge of normal pastoral activity" (*Novo Millennio Ineunte*, 29). As we have seen, neither John Paul II nor Pope Benedict XVI consider *normal* to mean "mediocre or static." *Normal* means to be constantly open to the guidance and "ever new irruptions of the Holy Spirit"—to be constantly in a state of renewal, particularly (in our day) striving to understand and live out the various dimensions of renewal called for by the Second Vatican Council. This is challenging but also exciting and enriching, if the challenge is embraced.

However, there are many misconceptions of this desired renewal. Some equate a renewed parish with a lot of frenetic and feverish activity. Yes, a renewed parish perhaps will have parishioners involved in many things (or intensely involved in a few things), but Pope John Paul II also indicated that renewed parishes will be "schools" of prayer (*Novo Millennio Ineunte*, 31) inevitably reflecting the depth of this prayer in its life.

Perhaps it is easier to describe what a renewed parish is *not*. It is said that a parish is a place where any Catholic can feel "at home." Unfortunately, this can be construed as a sort of "homogenized Catholicism" in which people cannot express their views, share their gifts, exercise their charisms, or venture to do something new. Instead of exhibiting the rich and vibrant diversity of the church, made up of "spiritually alive" Catholics seeking to grow in faith and holiness, parishes can easily become "havens of the humdrum," where people come to feel comfortable and secure, that is, not threatened by the challenge of the gospel or the call to renewal through the different streams and forms of renewal and grace present in the church in our time that are truly from the Lord.

Sadly, some parishes seem to be governed by the "eleventh commandment": "Don't rock the boat" (or its variations: "Don't change anything;" "We've always done it this way in our parish;" "Why do we need a renewal program, Bible study, adult education class, Life in the Spirit seminar, parish mission…?").

True, some forms of renewal might not be for the whole church or for every parish. They may be for a particular lay movement, religious community, or devotional group. Nonetheless, some forms of renewal, especially those (in our time) that are part of the teaching of the Second Vatican Council, are for the *whole* church and hence should find living expression in normal parish life: renewal of the liturgy and the sacraments, Scripture study, use of charisms, active lay participation, the pursuit of holiness, social concern and charitable works, and so on should not be the sole domain of voluntary groups or associations but rather part of the fabric of normal Catholic (that is, parish) life. How these are expressed in different parishes will vary, but church renewal means the insistence that no truly Catholic parish will neglect what the Lord is speaking and doing in the church in our time, as we are directed in this quest by the church's pastors.

In a dialogue with members of the Pontifical Council of the Laity on June 16, 1999, Cardinal Joseph Ratzinger spoke of the need for bishops and priests to be bold in helping the movements of God's grace in our time be integrated into the particular (local) churches and parishes. He said that they should "recognize their duty to see to it that the movements enter into the life of the diocese and the parish…to help 'normal' people, who perhaps find some unusual expressions of the movements a little bit odd: these people need to be helped to be generous, to let themselves be astonished by the various expressions found by the Holy Spirit."[21] I can't help but think of St. Peter on the Day of Pentecost explaining to the "normal" people, who thought that the expressions of him and the apostles were "a little bit odd," that this was the result of their being filled with the Holy Spirit: speaking in tongues and prophesying about the resurrection of Jesus. Peter had to explain that this same Spirit and these same gifts were for them as well, and for all who would come to believe in Jesus and be baptized!

Unfortunately, too often in diocesan and parish life, just the opposite happens: Those who want to bring their gifts into the mainstream of the life of the parish are told that they can't because the "normal" Catholics will not understand or will not accept them. "Thou shalt not rock the boat." And the church is not renewed. And those seeking to bring renewal to the church are marginalized: they can go do this in their own private group, perhaps, but not in the parish.

Let us instead follow the approach of Cardinal Ratzinger and heed the words of Pope John Paul II in *Novo Millennio Ineunte* about a "spirituality of communion":

> A spirituality of communion…means an ability to think of our brothers and sisters in faith within the profound unity of the Mystical Body, and therefore as "those who are part of me." This makes us able to share their joys and sufferings, to sense their desires and attend to their needs…. A spirituality of communion implies also the ability to see what is positive in others, to welcome it and prize it as a gift from God: not only as

a gift for the brother or sister who has received it directly, but also as a "gift for me." (*Novo Millennio Ineunte*, 43)

Pope Benedict on Discerning Renewal Movements

Church history teaches us that there are many ways that renewal movements and groups have been integrated into the church's life. Seldom has the best solution been simply to have members of a movement of renewal join a parish and "surrender" their grace or charism, if it is authentic. As Cardinal Ratzinger observed,

> movements appear in ever new forms in history—and necessarily so, because they are the Holy Spirit's answer to the ever changing situations in which the Church lives…. We must only be attentive to them. Using the gift of discernment, we must only learn to accept what is good in them, and discard what is bad.[22]

More specifically, the cardinal listed some criteria for what constitutes a genuine ecclesial movement in the church. These include

- "being rooted in the faith of the Church"
- "the wish to lead the *vita apostolica* [apostolic life]," which includes values such as "renunciation of property, celibacy, [and] the abandonment of any attempt to impose their own image of the Church"
- "apostolic activity [in which] pride of place is given…to the proclamation of the Gospel," especially to the poor, and not by word alone but by charity, which is the "inner source" of evangelization, the "mainspring of its truth and its action"
- "a deep, personal encounter with Christ," in which "the person is struck and penetrated by Christ to the depths of his or her being." Only among those so "touched in their innermost being…can true community grow."[23]

Finally his address turned to the "dangers" posed by renewal through movements. On the one hand Cardinal Ratzinger warned the movements against pride and exclusivity, that is, against a movement being "absolutised…identified with the Church herself," seeing itself not as "*one* of the many forms of Christian life" but "as the *one* way for everyone." On the other hand, the danger for the hierarchy and the local church is that they can fail to recognize the gift or the prophetic message that the movement brings to the church and consequently stifle the movement.

> [T]he local Churches, too, even the bishops, must be reminded that they must avoid any uniformity of pastoral organizations and programs. They must not turn their own pastoral plans into the criterion of what the Holy Spirit is allowed to do: an obsession with planning could render the Churches impervious to the action of the Holy Spirit, to the power of God by which they live. Not everything should be fitted into the straightjacket of a single uniform organization; what is needed is less organization and more spirit![24]

In sum, important lessons are to be learned both by members of ecclesial renewal movements and groups and by representatives of the institutional church. The Holy Spirit must educate all in humility, selflessness, and unity: "Both sides must learn from each other, allow themselves to be purified by each other, put up with each other, and discover how to attain those spiritual gifts of which St. Paul speaks in his great Hymn to Love (cf. *1 Cor* 13:4–7)."[25]

Cardinal Ratzinger concluded this address with words that echo the sentiments of Popes John XXIII, Paul VI, and John Paul II:

> After all these reflections and arguments, what should remain
> at the end is above all a feeling of gratitude and joy. Gratitude
> that the Holy Spirit is quite plainly at work in the Church and
> is lavishing new gifts on her in our time too, gifts through
> which she relives the joy of her youth (cf. Ps 42:4 *Vulgate*).
> Gratitude for the many people, young and old, who accept
> God's call and joyfully enter into the service of the Gospel
> without looking back. Gratitude for the bishops who open
> themselves up to the new movements, create room for them
> in their local Churches, struggle patiently with them in order
> to overcome their one-sidedness and guide them to the right
> form…. Christ lives, and he sends the Holy Spirit from the
> Father—that is the joyful and life-giving experience that is
> given to us by the meeting with the ecclesial [and all renewal]
> movements in our time.[26]

When Cardinal Joseph Ratzinger became Pope Benedict XVI, his
commitment to support ecclesial groups and movements of
renewal continued, building upon the work of his papal predecessors. Shortly after the pope's installation, Cardinal Angelo
Sodano, the Vatican's secretary of state, said that "Benedict XVI
will continue to guide with paternal affection the ecclesial movements, associations and communities which were nurtured by
Pope John Paul II."[27]

On Pentecost 2006 Pope Benedict followed Pope John Paul II's
example in inviting participants in these groups to Rome. He met
with their leaders, offering to all his encouragement, support, and
guidance. Throughout the years of both of these popes, the
Pontifical Council for the Laity has been directly and actively
involved in relating to and pastoring these groups, movements,

and communities church-wide. Its publication of *Movements in the Church, Proceedings of the World Congress of Ecclesial Movements, Rome, 27–29 May 1998* (1999) and *The Ecclesial Movements in the Pastoral Concern of Bishops* (2000), in the *Laity Today* series, reflects the progress being made in helping these movements achieve ecclesial maturity and understand more fully their role in the church's renewal.

Conclusion

In the early thirteenth century, God called a young Francis of Assisi to leave his affluent, worldly life and devote himself to rebuilding churches. Francis at that time had no idea how God was going to use him to renew the Catholic church. He also was unaware of the broader plan of God for this renewal that included Dominic Guzman and his preachers, St. Simon Stock and his Carmelites, and Clare of Assisi and other women and men of his time who would imitate him in living radical poverty out of love for Jesus Christ. He had no idea that this great groundswell of renewal grace would involve popes and cardinals and would culminate in a great council of the church's bishops, the Fourth Lateran Council. All that God desired Francis to do was to respond simply and in faith to his call, in humble obedience to Christ and his church.

It should surprise no one, at least no one with faith who knows church history, that God would give the grace of renewal in ever new ways as the church continues her pilgrim journey through history. We have noted in this chapter that this grace of renewal has blossomed and is blossoming once again in the Catholic church, especially in the aftermath of the Second Vatican Council. Blessed Pope John XXIII called the church to pray for a "New

Pentecost." All of the documents of that council gave directives aimed at spiritual as well as structural renewal of different aspects of the church: consecrated life, the bishops' pastoral office, priesthood and priestly formation, missionary activity, liturgy, and the apostolate of the laity, to name a few.

It is evident that the renewal actually called for by the Second Vatican Council in its documents has not always come about successfully or smoothly. The pastoral statements of the post–Vatican II popes (and many other pastors) have acknowledged this but also have echoed a common theme: The directives of the Second Vatican Council are the Holy Spirit's word to the church in our age, and we must continue to seek to implement them fully and faithfully, with the Lord's strength and guidance.

God has also blessed the church with the guidance of many wise pastors, especially many admirable popes. Let us be grateful and thank the Lord for his faithfulness and for all that his grace has accomplished. And may the Lord continue to bless, strengthen, and guide us, and the church, in this quest for renewal!

NOTES

Chapter One: What Is Renewal?

1. This translation is from *The Liturgy of the Hours* (New York: Catholic Book, 1976), Friday Morning Prayer, taken from *The Psalms: A New Translation* (London: The Grail, 1963).

2. John Paul II, Audience With the Council of the International Office of the Charismatic Renewal, December 11, 1979, as quoted in Kilian McDonnell, ed., *Open the Windows: The Popes and the Charismatic Renewal* (South Bend, Ind.: Greenlawn, 1989), pp. 25–26:

    [P]ermit me to explain my own charismatic life.

    I have always belonged to this renewal in the Holy Spirit. My own experience is very interesting. When I was in school, at the age of 12 or 13, sometimes I had difficulties in my studies…. My father gave me a book on prayer. He opened it to a page and said to me: "Here you have the prayer to the Holy Spirit. You must say this prayer every day of your life." I have remained obedient to this order that my father gave nearly 50 years ago…. This was my first spiritual initiation, so I can understand all the different charisms. All of them are part of the riches of the Lord.

Chapter Two: The Foundation of Renewal: Repentance and Prayer

1. Charles Grandison Finney, *Finney on Revival: The Highlights of the Sermons on Revival*, E.E. Shelhamer, ed. (Minneapolis: Bethany House, n.d.), p. 9.

2. Finney, pp. 17, 18.

3. Finney, p. 15.

4. Finney, p. 27.

5. Finney, p. 13.

6. Finney, p. 37.

7. Tertullian, "On Prayer," as quoted in *The Liturgy of the Hours*, vol. 2 (New York: Catholic Book, 1976), p. 250: "In the past prayer was able to bring down punishment, rout armies, withhold the blessing of rain. Now, however, the prayer of the just turns aside the whole anger of God, keeps vigil for its enemies, pleads for persecutors.... *Prayer is the one thing that can conquer God* [italics mine]. But Christ has willed that it should work no evil, and has given it all power over good."

8. See Finney, p. 37.

9. Sister Mary Bendyna, "Address to LCWR on Vocations to Religious Life Study," *Origins*, vol. 39, no. 12 (August 27, 2009), p. 202.

10. Bendyna, pp. 200–201. One example: the Dominican Congregation of St. Cecilia in Nashville, Tenn. accepted twenty-three postulants in 2009.

Chapter Three: Eschatological and Ecclesiological Perspectives

1. Extraordinary Synod of 1985, II, B, b.1.

2. Quoted in Avery Dulles, *A Church to Believe In: Discipleship and the Dynamics of Freedom* (New York: Crossroad, 1982), pp. 25, 33.

3. Quoted in Dulles, p. 33.

4. Dulles, pp. 25, 26.

5. Quoted in Edward D. O'Connor, *Pope Paul and the Spirit: Charisms and Church Renewal in the Teaching of Paul VI* (Notre Dame, Ind.: Ave Maria, 1978), p. 247.

6. Pope John Paul II, "Charisms Have a Role in the Church's Life," *L'Osservatore Romano*, English ed., July 1, 1992, p. 11.

7. Pope John Paul II, General audience, March 9, 1994, "Lay Charisms Build Up the Church," *L'Osservatore Romano*, English ed., March 16, 1994, p. 11.

8. Pope John Paul II, Address on the Occasion of the Meeting With the Ecclesial Movements and New Communities, Rome, May 30, 1998, no. 4, in *Movements in the Church: Proceedings of the World Congress of the Ecclesial Movements* (Vatican: Pontifical Council on the Laity, 1999), p. 221.

9. Bill McCarthy, ed., *The Holy Spirit in the Writings of Pope John Paul II* (McKees Rocks, Penn.: St. Andrew's Productions, 2001), p. 337. See Pope John Paul II's Address to Participants in the Second International Conference of Ecclesial Movements, March 2, 1987, *L'Osservatore Romano,* English ed., March 16, 1987, p.12).

10. Pope John Paul II, Message to Cardinal J. Francis Stafford on the Occasion of the Congress of the Catholic Laity, no. 4, November 21, 2000, available at www.vatican.va.

11. Pope Benedict XVI, *Regina Coeli* Address, May 15, 2005, available at www.vatican.va.

12. Pontifical Council for the Laity, "The Beauty of Being a Christian and the Joy of Communicating It," *News 2006*, available at www.vatican.va.

13. Pope Benedict XVI, Homily at Meeting With the Ecclesial Movements and New Communities, June 3, 2006, www.vatican.va.

14. Pope Benedict XVI, Address to the Members of Communion and Liberation Movement on the 25th Anniversary of Its Pontifical Recognition, March 24, 2007, available at www.vatican.va.

15. Karl Rahner, "Do Not Stifle the Spirit," *Theological Investigations*, vol. 7, David Bourke, trans. (New York: Herder & Herder, 1971), p. 73.

16. Rahner, p. 82.

17. Dulles, pp. 37–38.

18. See Joseph Carl Ratzinger, "The Ecclesial Movements," in *Movements in the Church*, pp. 25–29.

19. Ratzinger, "The Ecclesial Movements," p. 32.

Chapter Four: The Power of Personal Charism

1. T.S. Eliot, "Choruses from 'The Rock'," in *T.S. Eliot, Collected Poems, 1909–1962* (New York: Harcourt, Brace and World, 1963), p. 153.

2. Karl Rahner, "The Church of the Saints," in *Theological Investigations*, vol. 3, Karl H. and Boniface Kruger, trans. (Baltimore: Helicon, 1967), p. 104.

3. Dulles, p. 36.

4. Ratzinger, "The Ecclesial Movements," pp. 25–29.

5. Extraordinary Synod, II, A, 4.

6. Fidel González Fernández, "Charisms and Movements in the History of

the Church," *The Ecclesial Movements in the Pastoral Concern of Bishops* (Vatican City: Pontifical Council for the Laity, 2000), p. 82.

7. Fernández, pp. 81, 82.

8. Christopher M. Bellitto, *Renewing Christianity: A History of Church Reform from Day One to Vatican II* (New York: Paulist, 2001), pp. 72, 98.

9. Fernández, p. 86.

10. F.L. Cross and E.A. Livingstone, eds., *The Oxford Dictionary of the Christian Church*, 2nd ed. (New York: Oxford University Press, 1984), p. 162.

11. Bernard of Clairvaux, *Song of Songs 1*, vol. 2, *The Works of Bernard of Clairvaux* (Kalamazoo, Mich.: Cistercian, 1971), pp. 134, 136.

12. Bonaventure, "*Legenda Major*," in *Bonaventure* (New York: Paulist, 1978), pp. 191, 192.

13. Omer Englebert, *St. Francis of Assisi: A Biography* (Ann Arbor, Mich.: Servant, 1979), p. 67.

14. Bonaventure, p. 208.

15. Bonaventure, pp. 273, 274.

16. Bonaventure, p. 275.

17. Fernández, p. 90.

18. Fernández, p. 90.

19. *Oxford Dictionary*, pp. 253, 254; Cynthia Cavnar, *The Saints from A to Z* (Ann Arbor, Mich.: Servant, 2000), pp. 49, 50.

20. *Oxford Dictionary*, p. 198.

21. See *Oxford Dictionary*, pp. 198, 603.

22. *Oxford Dictionary*, p. 1239.

23. Owen Chadwick, *The Reformation* (Baltimore: Penguin, 1972), p. 256.

24. Henri Daniel-Rops, *The Catholic Reformation*, John Warrington, trans. (New York: E.P. Dutton, 1962), pp. 39, 40.

25. Daniel-Rops, pp. 43, 44.

26. Chadwick, pp. 260, 261.

27. John C. Olin, *The Catholic Reformation: Savanarola to Ignatius of Loyola* (New York: Fordham University Press, 1991), p. 198.

28. Ignatius had to solicit prayers and support among church leaders for the rule's approval, since there were so many groups clamoring for this

at the time. Only Ignatius' insistence on the uniqueness of his society, with support and prayers, finally achieved this outcome.

29. Fernández, p. 94.

30. *Oxford Dictionary*, p. 1350.

31. Cavnar, p. 197.

32. Ralph Martin, *The Fulfillment of All Desire* (Steubenville, Ohio: Emmaus Road, 2006), p. 20.

33. *Oxford Dictionary*, pp. 237, 238.

34. Chadwick, p. 254.

35. Antonio Gallonio, quoted in Paul Turks, *Philip Neri, The Fire of Joy* (New York: Alba House, 1995), pp. 16, 17.

36. Turks, pp. 17–18.

37. Ludwig Pastor, cited in Olin, p. 16.

38. Olin, p. 17.

39. Daniel-Rops, pp. 128–130.

40. "St. Philip Neri, Confessor—1515–1595," available at www.ewtn.com.

41. Turks, p. 125.

42. Turks, p. 23.

43. Bellitto, p. 177.

44. Bellitto, p. 183.

45. Fernández, pp. 97–99.

46. Jay P. Dolan, *Catholic Revivalism: The American Experience, 1830–1900* (Notre Dame, Ind.: University of Notre Dame Press, 1978), p. 95.

47. Dolan, pp. xv, xvi.

48. Dolan, p. 95.

49. Dolan, p. 48.

50. Dolan, p. 70.

51. A. Aufray, *St. John Bosco* (Bollington, Cheshire: St. Dominic Savio House, 1964), p. 99.

52. Aufray, p. 98.

53. G.K. Chesterton, *Orthodoxy: The Romance of Faith* (New York: Image, 1959), p. 101.

Chapter Five: The Influence of Ecclesial Office

1. *Oxford Dictionary*, p. 906.

2. *Oxford Dictionary*, pp. 1276, 1317.

3. Stephen B. Clark, *Unordained Elders and Renewal Communities* (New York: Paulist, 1976), pp. 6, 50–60.

4. Fernández, p. 83.

5. *Oxford Dictionary*, p. 154.

6. Bellitto, pp. 41, 42.

7. Bellitto, p. 49.

8. Fernández, p. 87.

9. See Fernández, p. 87.

10. *Oxford Dictionary*, p. 596.

11. Bellitto, p. 62. See H.E.J. Cowdrey, *Pope Gregory VII, 1073–1085* (Oxford: Clarendon, 1998).

12. *Oxford Dictionary*, p. 704.

13. Bellitto, p. 80.

14. Thomas of Celano, "The Remembrance of the Desire of a Soul," bk. 1, chap. 11, 17, *The Founder,* vol. 2, *Francis of Assisi: Early Documents* (New York: New City Press, 2000), p. 256.

15. Englebert, p. 59.

16. Jacques Paul Migne, *Patroligiae cursus completus, Series Latina*, vol. 216 (Paris: Petit Montrouge, 1891), pp. 73, 74, 75–77. Translations of the various quotations from this source are my own.

17. Chadwick, p. 266.

18. Quoted in Olin, p. 185.

19. Olin, pp. 271–272.

20. Olin, pp. 16–17.

21. Chadwick, p. 284.

22. Chadwick, pp. 284–285; *Oxford Dictionary*, p. 270.

23. Pius IX, Syllabus of Errors, available at www.papalencyclicals.net.

24. *Oxford Dictionary*, pp. 813, 814.

25. *Oxford Dictionary*, p. 814.

26. Val Gaudet, "A Woman and the Pope," *New Covenant*, October 1973, p. 5.

27. Gaudet, p. 5.

28. Gaudet, p. 6.

29. Guadet, p. 5.

Chapter Six: *Enthusiasm* Revisited

1. Christopher Dawson, "Religious Enthusiasm," review of *Enthusiasm* by Ronald Knox, *Month*, New Series 5, 1951, p. 8.
2. Ronald Knox, *Enthusiasm: A Chapter in the History of Religion* (Oxford: Clarendon, 1950), p. 589. Hereafter cited as "Knox."
3. Knox, p. v.
4. Knox, p. 1.
5. Ronald Knox, *A Spiritual Aeneid* (New York: Sheed & Ward, 1958), pp. 135, 138.
6. Ronald Knox and Arnold Lunn, *Difficulties: Being a Correspondence about the Catholic Religion between Ronald Knox and Arnold Lunn*, 3rd ed. (London: Eyre and Spottiswoode, 1958), p. 231.
7. Knox, p. 2.
8. Knox, p. 2.
9. Knox, p. 2.
10. Knox, p. 579.
11. See Knox, pp. 586–587.
12. Knox, p. 3.
13. Knox, p. 585.
14. Knox, pp. 585–587.
15. Knox, pp. 587–588.
16. Knox, p. 3.
17. Knox, p. 584.
18. Knox, pp. 3, 585.
19. Knox, p. 4.
20. Knox, p. 580.
21. Knox, p. 12.
22. Knox, pp. 14–15.
23. Knox, pp. 9–24.
24. Knox, p. 25.
25. Knox, p. 37.
26. Knox, p. 49.
27. Knox, pp. 8, 590.
28. Knox, p. 49.

29. Knox, p. 50.
30. Knox, p. 56.
31. Knox, p. 56.
32. Knox, pp. 60, 66.
33. Knox, p. 70.
34. Knox, p. 76.
35. Knox, p. 105.
36. Knox, p. 98.
37. Knox, p. 107.
38. Knox, p. 109.
39. Knox, p. 79.
40. Knox, p. 96.
41. Knox, p. 103.
42. Knox, p. 104.
43. Knox, p. 76.
44. Knox, p. 111.
45. Knox, pp. 110–111.
46. Knox, p. 112.
47. Knox, pp. 113–116.
48. Knox, p. 121.
49. Knox, pp. 120–126.
50. Knox, p. 123.
51. Knox, p. 131.
52. Knox, p. 135.
53. Knox, p. 134.
54. Knox, p. 137.
55. Knox, p. 140.
56. Knox, p. 147.
57. Knox, p. 152.
58. Knox, pp. 160–166, 167–168.
59. Knox, p. 5.
60. Dawson, p. 9.
61. Knox, p. 211.
62. Knox, p. 210.

63. Knox, p. 218.

64. Knox, p. 232.

65. See Knox, pp. 248–249, 590.

66. See Knox, pp. 245–247.

67. Knox, p. 350

68. Knox, p. 286.

69. Knox, p. 261.

70. See Knox, p. 352.

71. Knox, p. 359.

72. Knox, p. 364.

73. Knox, p. 365.

74. See Knox, p. 360.

75. See Knox, p. 371.

76. See Knox, p. 375.

77. Knox, p. 379.

78. Knox, p. 382.

79. See Knox, pp. 381–385.

80. Knox, p. 388.

81. See Knox, pp. 391, 397.

82. See Knox, p. 399.

83. See Knox, pp. 402–403.

84. See Knox, pp. 405–406.

85. Knox, p. 408.

86. See Knox, pp. 410, 413–417.

87. Knox, p. 412.

88. See Knox, p. 420.

89. Knox, p. 419.

90. Knox, p. 421.

91. Knox, p. 449.

92. Knox, p. 537.

93. Knox, p. 450.

94. Knox, pp. 451, 452.

95. Knox, p. 516.

96. See Knox, p. 515.

97. Knox, p. 452.

98. Howard Snyder, *The Radical Wesley & Patterns for Church Renewal* (Downer's Grove, Ill.: Inter-Varsity Press, 1980), pp. 102–103, 117, 123, 164.

99. Knox, p. 2.

100. See Knox, p. 549.

101. Knox, p. 550.

102. See Knox, p. 552.

103. Knox, p. 565.

104. Knox, p. 572.

105. See Knox, p. 570.

106. Knox, p. 577, quoting Hannah Whitall Smith, *Religious Fanaticism* (London: Faber & Gwyer, 1928), p. 165.

107. Knox, p. 577.

108. Knox, pp. v, vi.

109. Knox, p. 590.

110. Knox, p. v.

111. Knox, p. 104; see pp. 76, 426.

112. Knox, p. 2.

113. Knox, pp. 590–591.

114. In my unpublished doctoral dissertation, "Ronald Knox's Theory of Enthusiasm and Its Application to the Catholic Charismatic Renewal," Toronto, Canada, 1979, I apply Knox's criteria to the Catholic charismatic renewal movement.

Chapter Seven: Renewal in the Twentieth and Twenty-first Centuries

1. You may have noticed that this book has not discussed "programs" for the renewal of the church. Although these may have some value, neither Jesus, nor St. Francis, nor many of the saints who renewed the church did so by implementing a program, though they certainly each had an approach to God and to the kingdom of God or the church that they sought to follow, and they did have followers who sought to imitate and learn from their lives. Perhaps the rules of religious life that some founders developed could be considered "programs."

2. Cardinal Joseph Ratzinger, *The Ratzinger Report: an Exclusive Interview on the State of the Church*, Salvator Attanasio and Graham Harrison, trans. (San Francisco: Ignatius, 1985), pp. 30, 31.

3. As an example of this, the Catholic church up to the time of the Second Vatican Council was still often referred to as the Tridentine church, because its life was still decisively shaped by the Council of Trent of the sixteenth century.

4. First Homily of His Holiness Benedict XVI, at the End of the Eucharistic Concelebration With the Cardinal Electors in the Sistine Chapel, April 20, 2005, available at catholicnews.com.

5. *Ratzinger Report*, p. 31.

6. Pope Benedict XVI, First Homily.

7. Extraordinary Synod, II, B, b. 1.

8. Extraordinary Synod, II, B, b. 1.

9. Extraordinary Synod, II, C, 1.

10. Joseph Ratzinger, "Ecclesial Movements," pp. 49, 50.

11. Ratziner, "Ecclesial Movements," p. 50.

12. Ratzinger, "Ecclesial Movements," p. 50.

13. In my book *Your Life in the Holy Spirit: What Every Catholic Needs to Know and Experience* (Ijamsville, Md.: Word Among Us, 2007), I discuss how unity or communion is the "most reliable sign of the presence of the Holy Spirit" in a group or community within the church. Unity is at the heart of God's plan for the church, and it cannot be counterfeited (see pp. 162–163).

14. Pope John Paul II, Address to Members of Ecclesial Communities, May 30, 1998, as quoted in *L'Osservatore Romano,* English ed., June 3, 1998, p. 2.

15. Pope Benedict XVI's Address at the Opening of the Ecclesial Convention of the Diocese of Rome, "Lay people in the Church: from collaboration to 'co-responsibility,'" *L'Osservatore Romano,* English ed., June 3, 2009, p. 4.

16. *Ratzinger Report*, pp. 43, 44.

17. Ratzinger, "Ecclesial Movements," pp. 46, 47.

18. Pope John Paul II, Address to Members of Ecclesial Communities, p. 2.

19. Ratzinger, "Ecclesial Movements," p. 24.

20. Ratzinger, "Ecclesial Movements," pp. 24, 25.

21. Ratzinger, in *The Ecclesial Movements in the Pastoral Concern of the Bishops*, pp. 232, 233.

22. Ratzinger, "Ecclesial Movements," p. 46.

23. Ratzinger, "Ecclesial Movements," pp. 48, 49.

24. Ratzinger, "Ecclesial Movements," pp. 49, 50.

25. Ratzinger, "Ecclesial Movements," p. 50.

26. Ratzinger, "Ecclesial Movements," p. 51.

27. Zenit Online News Service, April 26, 2005.

INDEX

ABOUT THE AUTHOR

ALAN SCHRECK, PH.D., is a professor of theology at Franciscan University of Steubenville in Ohio and the author of numerous books, including *Catholic and Christian, The Essential Catholic Catechism, Catholic and Christian for Young Adults, Vatican II: The Crisis and the Promise,* and *The Compact History of the Catholic Church.* Dr. Schreck and his wife, Nancy, are the parents of five children.